The Battle of The River Plate

The First Naval Battle of the Second World War

Dedicated
To the Men who Brought us
Victory

The Battle of The River Plate

The First Naval Battle of the Second World War

Gordon Landsborough

Frontline Books

THE BATTLE OF THE RIVER PLATE
The First Naval Battle of the Second World War

First published in 1956 by Panther Books, London.

This edition published in 2016 by Frontline Books,
an imprint of Pen & Sword Books Ltd,
47 Church Street, Barnsley, S. Yorkshire, S70 2AS

ISBN: 978-1-47387-895-2

CIP data records for this title are available from the British Library

For more information on our books, please visit
www.frontline-books.com, email **info@frontline-books.com**
or write to us at the above address.

Printed and bound by CPI Group (UK) Ltd, Croydon, CR0 4YY
Typeset in 10.5/13 point Palatino

Contents

The Despatch on the Battle of the River Plate which was submitted to the Lords Commissioners of the Admiralty, by Rear Admiral H.H. Harwood, KCB, OBE, Rear Admiral Commanding South American Division, on 30 December 1939.

Long Ago

It was 1937, the time of the Coronation of His Majesty King George VI. Off Spithead the might of British naval seapower was massing for review in honour of the new king, and with them were ships representative of the navies of other nations.

One afternoon, in glorious sunshine, two warships found themselves steaming along the Channel towards Spithead. One was the German battleship *Admiral Graf Spee*, the very latest addition to Hitler's navy. The other was a British cruiser, *Achilles*.

The *Admiral Graf Spee* crammed on speed and tried to race the smaller warship to Spithead, and *Achilles* took up the challenge.

Achilles won.

Acknowledgements

My thanks to the Admiralty: to the Chief of Naval Information's Office for their assistance, and Mr. G.H. Hurford, Historical Section, for his patience and courtesy in supplying the maps and reports which form the basis of this work.

To Commander A.B. Campbell, Lord Strabolgi, and Dudley Pope, whose books, all of the same title – *The Battle of the River Plate* – have also been referred to.

And to the veterans of the Battle of the River Plate whom I had the honour to meet in Plymouth – thirsty men who told me more than they realised ... men who should not be forgotten. Good fellows, *they* wrote the Battle of the River Plate.

List of Maps

Introduction

A t the outbreak of the Second World War the seas were the
highways of the world. Almost all intercontinental trade
around the globe was conducted by ships, great and small.
Protecting Britain's maritime activities was the Royal Navy's
primary role, in peace and in war, just as it was her enemies'
objective to disrupt those activities.

With the commencement of hostilities in 1939, the Royal
Navy sought to destroy the German Navy's ability to interfere
with Britain's merchant shipping. The main threats, it was
believed, came from submarines and surface raiders. In terms
of the latter, it was the powerful German capital ships which
were of the greatest concern to the Admiralty.

Enormous effort, in terms of time and resources, was put
into neutralising these ships, and the stories of their
destruction are some of the most exciting tales of the war. The
first of these was the operation to sink the German
Deutschland-class heavy cruiser *Admiral Graf Spee*, which
culminated in the Battle of the River Plate in December 1939.

Every movement by the British and Commonwealth ships
that chased and engaged *Admiral Graf Spee* is recorded in Rear
Admiral H.H. Harwood's report. This culminated with these
words written on Sunday, 17 December 1939, as the Royal
Navy warships sailed past the burning wreck of *Admiral Graf
Spee* in the estuary of the River Plate: "It was now dark, and

she was ablaze from end to end, flames reaching almost as high as the top of her control tower, a magnificent and most cheering sight."

Harwood also included with his despatch a list of observations drawn from the fighting with *Admiral Graf Spee*. This had been the first battle with a capital ship that the Royal Navy had been engaged in since the end of the First World War. Possibly his most enlightening comment was on the performance of *Admiral Graf Spee*'s captain, *Kapitän zur See* Hans Langsdorff.

When the pursuing British warships were spotted by *Admiral Graf Spee*, the German cruiser immediately turned towards them at full speed. This was quite illogical. *Admiral Graf Spee*'s 11-inch guns far outranged the 8-inch and 6-inch guns of the British cruisers. With a maximum speed of almost thirty knots, *Admiral Graf Spee* was only marginally slower than the British cruisers and so could have kept out of their range for a considerable time, enabling its heavier guns to inflict serious damage on the pursuers. But by closing the distance so quickly, the guns of the British cruisers were soon brought into range. Though *Admiral Graf Spee* struck and disabled HMS *Exeter* and put HMS *Ajax*'s aft gun turrets out of action, by the time the battle was discontinued, *Admiral Graf Spee* had been hit approximately seventy times.

As is well known, the damage caused to the German cruiser induced Langsdorff to put into Montevideo, the capital city of neutral Uruguay, for repairs. It was the end of her operational career, in which she accounted for 50,089 tons of Allied shipping.

John Grehan

Chapter 1

The First Victim

The first victim was the S.S. *Clement*, Booth Line, 5,050 tons, an ocean-going tramp steamer bound for Bahia, Salvador. It was September 30, 1939; the time mid-morning. The weather was good, the Brazilian coast west of them; they were near to yet another journey's end for the old ship, with nothing to tell them that within minutes they were to be involved by the hazards of war.

Third Officer H.J. Gill was on watch when the lookout called, "Ship on the port bow." Gill trained his glasses on the horizon and studied the distant vessel.

For over three weeks now his country and Germany had been at war. True, so far as the *Clement* was concerned, the declaration of war had made no difference to them – no submarines had chased them, no aircraft or armed merchant raiders had gunned them. War seemed remote here, off the coast of South America, not really comprehendible, something which in their hearts they discounted. The sun shone, the day was glorious. Though their ship zig-zagged, as a gesture to war-time safety demands, no one really believed that war could come to them so soon after the declaration of hostilities.

But – "Ship on the port bow!" A good officer took no chances. Now Gill kept his glasses on the distant vessel, waiting until it came close enough to be identified. He didn't have long to wait. The unknown ship was heading straight for them, and they could tell she was travelling at high speed by the way she came over the horizon.

About 11.15 the Third Officer picked up the speaking tube and called the ship's master, Captain F.C.P. Harris, who had just gone below to his cabin. "Captain, there's a man-o'-war bearing down on us fast, about four points on the port bow."

"I'll come right up."

Captain Harris quickly climbed to the bridge and looked towards the approaching warship. It was still several miles distant, and because it was bow on to them was difficult to identify. It was making no signals and they were unable to discern any flag.

Captain Harris said, "It could be the *Ajax*." It didn't seem possible for an enemy warship to be at large, with the might of the Royal Navy between them and Germany. And H.M.S. *Ajax* was known to be in South American waters.

For a few minutes the two officers watched the approach of the warship, still trying to identify it. It was throwing up enormous bow waves, so that Gill estimated – "She must be making thirty knots."

Captain Harris said, "Looks as though we're going to have visitors. Put up the ensign. I'll put on another jacket." He went below. He still believed the approaching vessel to be the *Ajax*, racing in at speed, probably hoping that she had intercepted a German merchantman who would scuttle herself if given enough time to do so.

When Captain Harris returned to the bridge, smart now in a clean white uniform jacket, the unknown warship was only three or four miles away and looking huge in the clear light of the tropical sun. But still she flew no flag and made no signal to them. It was beginning to be perplexing, and perhaps at that moment unease came to the watching officers.

Someone on the deck below shouted, "A plane's taking off!"

A seaplane suddenly hurtled off the deck of the warship, catapulted into the air. But the *Ajax* also had a seaplane …

The Chief Officer came running up as the seaplane swept round towards them. He asked his captain, "Shall we show our name board?" Captain Harris nodded and the Chief Officer started away. He had only moved a few paces when the plane came roaring down at them. Fascinated, officers and crew stared up at the noisy aircraft as it began to dive the length of the ship.

Then things began to happen at bewildering speed. Woodwork seemed to erupt and splinter around the officers on the bridge. They heard the rattle of a machine-gun above the deafening roar as the aircraft shot by overhead.

They caught a glimpse of markings under the wings of the seaplane. They were German, and the plane was strafing them with machine-gun fire.

Captain Harris heard Chief Officer Jones exclaim, "My God, it's a Jerry!" The *Clement*'s master was already stopping the ship. There wasn't a gun aboard, and that was all he could do in an effort to save their lives. "Shall I get the boats ready, sir?" the Chief Officer asked.

Captain Harris nodded, though his eyes were set grimly upon the seaplane. It was turning, heading straight for them again. "All hands on deck," the captain ordered, "And swing out those boats."

The ship was losing speed, and it should have been noticeable to the pilot of the aircraft, but it seemed to make no difference to him. He dived upon the ship again, raking it with machine-gun bullets. The Chief Officer staggered suddenly and blood spurted from his right hand and forearm. On deck men were shouting their anger at the attacker, and racing to get the boats into the water.

Again the seaplane came round, and again bullets flailed the boat-deck and bridge. But now they were ready for it and dived for cover, so that no one was hurt this time as it passed, though the wheelhouse was wrecked by bullets.

Below, following upon an instant instruction from Captain

Harris, the radio operator had begun to send out a distress signal. It began "RRR." That was a code signal meaning, "I am being attacked by aircraft." The operator managed to get out the ship's position before a signal went up on the battleship – "Stop. No wireless transmitting."

Captain Harris had no alternative but to obey. He could see 11-inch guns trained upon them, sufficient to blow them out of the water if he so much as hesitated. He ordered the radio operator up on deck and shouted to the crew to get into the boats and abandon ship. The *Clement* was going to be destroyed, and he knew it. The one consoling feature was that their message had got through; the wireless operator reported that his signal had been picked up by a Brazilian steamer, which presumably would relay it and bring help up to them.

Hurriedly putting the ship's confidential papers into a special weighted canvas bag, Captain Harris disposed of them over the side and then joined his men in one of the boats. As they pulled away, a piquet boat came across from the battleship. Silently, sullenly, the British seamen looked into the faces of enemy sailors. Young men, they were, flushed and excited by their victory. They took the *Clement*'s captain and Chief Engineer aboard, and returned them to the abandoned tramp. The Britishers would open the sea valves and scuttle the ship, the Germans told them. Obligingly, Chief Engineer Bryant opened some valves but they only flooded the ballast tanks and hours later the *Clement* had to be sunk by 6-inch gunfire from the battleship.

The Germans, in spite of their gun-strafing episode, were most courteous to their first victims. They radioed, "Please save the lifeboats of the *Clement*, 0945 south, 3404 west." The call was picked up and the following day one of the lifeboats was found by a Brazilian steamer. Three other lifeboats landed at Maceio the day after. Captain Harris and Mr. Bryant were put aboard a Greek vessel, the *Papalemos*, by the German warship commander which left them at the Cape Verde islands on October 9.

Soon reports were winging their way to the Admiralty in London. A pocket battleship, the *Admiral Scheer*, had claimed her first victim of World War II, unexpectedly in South American waters.

The officers and crew of the *Clement* knew it was the *Admiral Scheer*, for that name had been on the hat-bands of the German sailors in the piquet boat and aboard the warship. More, it was the name painted on the bows and stern of the German raider. Undoubtedly the pocket battleship was the *Admiral Scheer*.

And so began a deception by the enemy that was to puzzle the British Admiralty for over two months.

Chapter 2

The Hunt Begins

Within hours of the distress call from the *Clement*, word was flashed to a not altogether unprepared Admiralty in Whitehall that a British merchant ship had been sunk by enemy action off the coast of Brazil. At first that was all they knew – just that the *Clement* had been sunk – but whether by armed merchantman or something more formidable was not known until October 2. Then a dramatic message was radioed by the Brazilian ship which had picked up one of the *Clement*'s lifeboats that the Atlantic raider was the German pocket battleship, the *Admiral Scheer*. A pocket battleship, one of Hitler's not-so-secret weapons, was loose in the South Atlantic and on the rampage. It was grim news, though expected by the British Admiralty. The design of the ships had indicated their rôle in an eventual war, and long before the outbreak of hostilities tactics had been evolved to counter, so far as possible, the maraudings of the big, powerfully armed German raiders.

Not forgotten in the memory of Their Lords of the Admiralty was the success of the German raider, *Emden*, in the 1914-18 war. By November 9, 1914, this solitary light cruiser had accounted for no less than sixteen merchant ships in the Indian Ocean and Bay of Bengal, a total of 66,146 tons. She also captured and released one Allied and twelve neutral ships, with a total tonnage of 53,000.

All that was achieved by a comparatively small ship, insignificant in size compared with the pocket battleships, and with nowhere near the same formidable armament. The *Emden* had a displacement of 3,592 tons only, carrying ten 4.1-inch guns, and with a maximum speed of 24 knots. If a ship as small and as slow as that could wreak such havoc in such a short time, what appalling damage to the Allied war effort could Hitler's pocket battleships do? That was the worry in the Admiralty even before the declaration of war, but fortunately the great British public was not asked to share it.

True, the *Emden* had had a short life, being finally brought to action by the Australian cruiser, *Sydney*, 5,600 tons, armed with eight 6-inch guns, and outspeeding the German by two knots. The *Sydney's* superior firepower quickly disposed of the raider, but experts did not feel that the pocket battleships could so easily be tracked down and sunk.

They weren't designed to be tracked down easily, and they had a firepower which said their opponents would sink first if it came to a battle. It wasn't altogether the problem of search that worried the Admiralty, however – and to locate a fast-moving battleship in the vast expanse of an ocean was a proposition not lightly to be entertained. It was what happened when she was located.

For in all the British Navy were only three battle cruiser – Hood, Repulse *and* Renown *– considered fast enough and powerful enough to take on a pocket battleship with any hope of success . . . in the combined fleets of France and Britain, there were only five of such might. If other ships sought and found them, advisers told Hitler, they would merely commit suicide; for the pocket battleships could out-range and out-gun anything fast enough to come up with them, and were so heavily armoured it seemed they were invulnerable.*

The pocket battleship was the logical answer to attempts by Allied Powers to keep Germany, between the two world wars, in an inferior position so far as sea power was concerned. If Germany was not to be allowed a fleet of big and powerful ships, then what she built would outclass any comparable ships in the world. Thus the German Naval Chief, Grand Admiral Erich Raeder, caused the pocket battleships, as they became known, to be built, and accordingly he introduced a new factor into the calculations of opposing sea powers.

German naval power had been destroyed in the 1914-1918 war. In 1914 her fleet had been the second most powerful in the world, but defeat left her with only six obsolete battleships of the Deutschland type – her more modern warships being ordered into Scapa Flow when a humbled Germany applied for Armistice, later to be scuttled by their own crews rather than permit them to be taken over by the British and Allies.

The trouble began with the signing of peace terms between the warring nations. France, who knew more than any other country the horrors of war, wanted total German disarmament, but Britain, uneasy about the new republic of Russia, wanted to keep a partially armed Germany to act as a bulwark to any Communist moves westward.

The usual compromise was effected and the celebrated (in some eyes, notorious) Treaty of Versailles agreed to. Germany was not to be allowed to build or maintain submarines – Britain also insisted on that. She could, however, maintain a small surface fleet to protect her if attacked in the Baltic by Russia. This would consist of the six pre-dreadnought, obsolete battleships referred to, six light cruisers and a few torpedo boats. The Treaty of Versailles prohibited the building by Germany of any warships displacing more than 10,000 tons, such warships being expected to be coast-defence in character.

In fact for about a decade the Germans did not attempt to build any warships up to this limit, suffering as they were as a result of the long and terrible war, sick with defeat and torn inwardly by political parties seeking to gain power.

It was during this time that the victorious Powers also voluntarily imposed limitations on their own naval programmes, to prevent an armaments race which would cripple the economy of the countries concerned. In 1921, representatives of five sea powers, Britain, the United States, France, Japan and Italy, met at a Naval Conference in Washington, where they agreed to certain restrictions in the building of new warships. Each, it was decided, would retain their big battleships and battle-cruisers, but would in future not build cruisers exceeding 10,000 tons displacement. This put them on a level with the German limitations, but with an important difference, as will be seen later.

It is true that at a later conference the Big Five sea powers agreed to the building among themselves of certain battleships, but here it was decided that no war vessel *below* a certain tonnage would be laid down. Admiral Raeder's post-war naval policy was to provide Germany with battleships which appeared to conform to the 10,000-ton limitations, but which, in fact, were between the conventional cruiser of that size and the more powerful battleships. The result – his pocket battleships occupied a unique position.

Raeder wanted the best of two worlds and he saw that he got it.

While at first these five sea Powers made no restriction upon the number of cruisers which might be built, within the limitations stated, in 1930 and again in 1935 they also agreed to limit the number of cruisers armed with 8-inch guns. All this especially suited Britain, who had a greater need for numbers of smaller warships rather than for a few mighty battleships; but though the limitations thus imposed were laudable in their intention to save tax-payers' money, they gave a further advantage to the unscrupulous, power-crazy German dictator.

Even before Hitler came to power, however, the Germans had begun to build ships which were an evasion of the terms agreed to in the signing of the Treaty of Versailles. Ostensibly they complied with the agreed limit of 10,000 tons displacement, but very soon naval experts began to suspect that, in fact, Germany had built in excess of that tonnage.

In 1929 a vessel was laid down to replace one of the old Deutschland-class dreadnoughts, doomed for the scrap-heap. She was, in fact, to be named *Deutschland*. In 1931 Admiral Raeder began the construction of a second replacement vessel, the *Admiral Scheer*, and in 1932 work was begun on a third warship, the *Admiral Graf Spee*.

These three ships astonished the world when they were launched – ominously flying the flag of the new German Republic, the swastika, incidentally. They were far ahead of contemporary warships in design, and were immediately recognised as upsetting conventional naval strategy.

Each vessel had cost £3,750,000 to build, a fantastic amount by 1930 standards to spend on a warship of such size and, in defiance of the Versailles Treaty, their displacement approached 13,000 tons rather than remaining within the 10,000-ton limit agreed to.

But it was not so much their size that caused them to be dubbed "pocket battleships" as the power that was concentrated within their 609-foot hulls – hulls welded, incidentally, and using aluminium wherever possible. No old-fashioned riveting for Admiral Raeder!

In place of the conventional steam turbines, the pocket battleships packed 54,000 horsepower diesel engines, capable of 10,000 miles cruising at 15 knots before refuelling, and with a speed, remarkable for ships of their size, of 27.7 knots.

But it was their armament which staggered the naval experts. The pocket battleships carried six 11-inch guns mounted in two triple turrets, eight 5.9-inch guns, six 4-inch anti-aircraft guns and eight torpedo tubes. They also carried two aircraft which could be catapulted from their decks. Their deck and side armour was remarkably thick, so much so that it was not considered possible for the shells of our 8-inch cruisers to be able to penetrate it, except at very close range.

They had the firepower and defensive armour of a battleship, with the speed and manœuvrability of a large cruiser. As Raeder boasted at the time, they could out-sail any more powerful ship, and out-gun anything that could catch up with them.

Clearly they were designed for a purpose. That purpose – to make up for the limitations in naval strength of post-war Germany ... to make a few powerful ships serve the purpose of many.

Unlike the beginning of World War I, Germany entered the second world war of her choice with a very inferior navy, and quite obviously she discounted this arm of her forces (except for submarines), pinning her faith for the third time within a century on the might and resource of a finely equipped land army. Hitler appears to have allocated to the small German Navy of 1939 a diversionary rôle, and the purpose of the pocket battleships was to tie up the attentions of a disproportionately large part of the mighty British and French navies.

Again apart from submarines, of which Hitler probably had about eighty, in 1939 the German Navy consisted of two medium-sized battlecruisers, *Scharnhörst* and *Gneisenau*, built by Hitler in defiance of the Versailles Treaty, the three pocket battleships, two heavy cruisers – the *Blücher* and *Admiral Hipper* – and half a dozen 6-inch cruisers, as well as some armed merchantmen. The 45,000-ton *Bismarck* and *Tirpitz* were under construction, as was the 8-inch heavy cruiser *Prinz Eugen* and other ships. Germany had no aircraft carriers, but was building two.

Numerically the fleets of the United Kingdom and of France were vastly superior to Hitler's, but they were orthodox in design and therein lay an advantage to the German dictator. However, the combined French and British fleets totalled 21 capital ships (battleships and battle-cruisers), 59 cruisers, and a host of light cruisers, destroyers, sloops, etc., as well as aircraft carriers. Though many of these ships were old and out of date for a modem war, nevertheless Germany had to consider the fact that she was numerically at a considerable disadvantage. Britain especially still ruled the waves.

This dictated Germany's naval preparations for the war Hitler wanted, influencing the design of all the ships built, though most noticeably in the construction of the powerful pocket battleships. The *Deutschland*, *Admiral Scheer* and *Admiral Graf Spee* were cast in the rôle of wolves of the sea, and admirably designed for the purpose.

Before the outbreak of war, Admiral Raeder secretly dispatched his pocket battleships to be "lost" in the world's oceans, ready in case the war spread to other countries after Hitler's invasion of Poland. To maintain the pocket battleships at sea, he had tankers and supply ships stationed in strategic areas, so that the marauders could re-fuel and provision themselves and so maintain themselves away from land bases for months, or more than a year if need be.

Out at sea when war was declared, his pocket battleships knew their orders. They were to harry the ships that were vital to the enemy economy, especially to Britain, that island dependent upon the world for so much of her raw materials and foodstuffs.

But the British Admiralty knew the German battleships were out, and knew what to expect from them when war started, so, months ahead of the outbreak of war, they worked on a plan to out-wit and defeat the enemy when the emergency arose. It proved to be a most difficult task. Because of the strength of the pocket battleships, it meant that the search for them had to be conducted by groups of ships, so that if our faster but less powerful ships sighted the battleships, courage, seamanship and a concentration of gunfire might off-set the advantages of the bigger warships.

What was not easily explained, however, was how our ships could get close enough to hurt the thickly armoured Germans without being blown out of the water first. The pocket battleships' 11-inch guns outranged those of British and French cruisers by several miles, and, according to Raeder's theory, even if they were overtaken by a superior force, the battleships could pick off their opponents at leisure from a distance out of effective range of their opponents' 6-inch or 8-inch guns – like a boxer with superior reach holding off an opponent and playing with him.

That was the problem facing the British and French navies, but nevertheless hunting groups of warships were ready even before the outbreak of war, waiting for the pocket battleships to start their killing rôle, and hoping then for the good luck to come up with them.

Unknown to the experts was the fact that the pocket battleships were equipped with the German equivalent of radar. It was crude compared with modern day apparatus, inefficient and prone to break down, but it gave the German raiders a wonderful advantage over their unequipped opponents, in that they could "see" far over the horizon in every direction around them.

It seemed impossible even for hunting groups ever to come up with a raider who could see them from a great distance and take steps to avoid them.

Only the *Admiral Scheer* had ever been seen in action. This was in 1937. The *Deutschland* had been bombed while off Spanish waters by a Republican aircraft, which caused the death of several of the crew. On May 29, as a reprisal, the *Admiral Scheer* was ordered to shell the undefended town of Almeria, which she did, rendering 8,000 homeless and causing injury as well as a vast amount of damage.

This was hailed by the Germans, just getting into their stride so far as propaganda was concerned, as a glorious

THE BATTLE OF THE RIVER PLATE

victory. Later they were to make similar claims about the Battle of the River Plate, again with doubtful accuracy.

When the first raider report came through, the British Admiralty were not certain for some days as to whether the attacker had been a pocket battleship or one of the several armed German merchant cruisers known to be in the South Atlantic. Indeed, even after the reports came through from the survivors, picked up at sea in their lifeboat by the Brazilian ship, the confusion persisted for a while because of the remarkably contradictory character made of some of the descriptions of the enemy. However, in time it began to be accepted that it was a pocket battleship which had started to run amok in the waters off South America.

Very quickly after this, unfortunately, came another report to cast doubt upon the identity and possible position of the raider. It was learned that an attack had been made by a pocket battleship upon a Norwegian merchantman, the S.S. *Lorentz W. Hansen*, three hundred miles east of Newfoundland. The report of the crew was that the battleship was the *Deutschland*, but a suspicious Naval Intelligence wondered if perhaps this might not be the same battleship which had sunk the unfortunate S.S. *Clement* …

It was some time before they were to know the truth – that it wasn't the same pocket battleship, and that in fact two German warships were roving the Atlantic in search of prey.

The *Rawalpindi* was the next victim of the *Deutschland*, to continue briefly the history of that ship. The *Rawalpindi*, an armed British merchantman, completely out-gunned, nevertheless gallantly went for the German raider when she was attacked, damaging her somewhat with her small guns and finally sinking in action with her colours flying. After that the *Deutschland* made a run for home down the neutral coast of Norway – a favourite expedient with German home-bound ships.

Again, the British Naval Intelligence was puzzled by the report that the *Admiral Scheer* was active in South American waters, because according to their information that ship was in German waters.

Deutschland or *Admiral Scheer*, however, the hunt was on. A raider was loose on the high seas and affecting British interests. That raider had to be put out of the way and quickly, too.

So began a man-hunt – a hunt for an enemy man-o'-war – probably the biggest the world had ever seen. Yet days passed into weeks before the British Admiralty received any further report about the raider's activities, though in that time the mighty pocket battleship had continued at her work of waylaying and sinking merchant ships in the South Atlantic.

Chapter 3

Newton Beech

It was dawn in the South Atlantic – the day, October 5, less than a week after the sinking of the *Clement*. Captain J. Robison, master of the *Newton Beech,* a 3,000-ton ship owned by Ridley, Son & Tully of Newcastle-on-Tyne, had received a report that an enemy battleship, the *Admiral Scheer*, had started operations in southern waters, and his look-outs were vigilant.

They were north of St. Helena, that lonely speck in the middle of the Atlantic, carrying a cargo of maize en route from Cape Town to the UK. A 4-inch gun had been fitted at Cape Town, but Captain Robison rightly discounted it as an asset if they ran into a marauding pocket battleship. Instead he merely hoped to continue his way without sight of any hostile ship, and because the last report of the raider had placed it near to the coast of Brazil, a good thousand miles away, he was not unduly pessimistic.

He was asleep in his bunk when his Chief Officer called him from the bridge. It was about six o'clock. "There's a man-o'-war coming up fast," he was told, and because of the recent *Clement* episode, Captain Robison hastened to the bridge in his pyjamas.

He saw a warship travelling at speed, throwing up a huge bow wave, and heading straight for them. It was about six miles away. Captain Robison's first thought was – "She isn't

British," and was suspicious immediately. He ordered his Radio Officer to stand by, ready to transmit a warning signal if the battleship proved hostile, then he ran below to change out of his pyjamas. He had a feeling that his normal clothing might serve him better in the days to come.

Returning, he was so little sure of their prospects that he dumped his secret documents overboard before even identifying the oncoming vessel. When he reached the bridge, the warship was almost abeam, and he recognised her as the pocket battleship, the *Graf Spee*. His immediate thought was that *two* pocket battleships were loose in the Atlantic and he ordered his Radio Operator to begin his signal of distress. Three times the call went out, and then the German ship signalled for them to stop transmitting or they would fire upon the *Newton Beech*.

Regretfully, Captain Robison obeyed the command; equally, because he recognised the folly of such a procedure, he ordered his men not to fire the 4-inch gun. A popgun against such a foe would merely begin an unnecessary slaughter.

A surprise was in store for the British seamen, however, for the *Newton Beech* was not immediately sunk but put under a German prize crew and made to follow the raider. Captain Robison's suspicions were aroused, and he spoke to the German officers aboard, saying casually he had heard over the radio that the *Graf Spee* had sunk the *Clement* days earlier. Immediately the Germans denied all knowledge of the *Clement*, and for a while Captain Robison felt he had been mistaken in his suspicions.

Next day, however, a motorboat came alongside the smaller vessel and Captain Robison was ordered into it for interview with the *Graf Spee*'s captain. Aboard the battleship he was taken below and introduced to Captain Hans Langsdorff. It was a very courteous meeting; the German commander, one of the old school, being most punctilious in his reception of his prisoner.

For a while they talked, and then, quite unexpectedly, Langsdorff said, "My officers tell me you believe the *Graf Spee* to have sunk another British ship?"

For some reason Captain Robison decided to stick to his story, and very casually said, yes, it had been broadcast by the Admiralty that the *Graf Spee* had sunk the *Clement*. His story must have sounded very convincing, for almost immediately Langsdorff shrugged and admitted it to be true. They had attacked their first victim under the name of their sister ship, the *Admiral Scheer*, he agreed, though he didn't explain why.

Captain Robison, detained now aboard the *Graf Spee*, made his own guesses. War is a game of bluff. Langsdorff's actions were designed to confuse the enemy and ultimately to cause them to waste their strength by looking for a ship which was not there.

At the time, British Naval Intelligence had wondered that the crew of the first ship to be sunk by a German battleship should be allowed to get safely ashore with their information. It seemed bad strategy to announce that an enemy warship had started operations in the South Atlantic, and Captain Robison was the first to comprehend why it had been done.

Langsdorff's intention, it became clear later, was to appear elsewhere as the *Graf Spee* (in fact he did, in the Indian Ocean, where he allowed another ship's crew to get ashore with the news that the *Graf Spee* was on the rampage along Africa's east coast). Thus the forces opposed to Germany would be deployed to meet the threat of two battleships and not one, with a consequent wastage of ships and manpower, diverted from areas which could not reasonably have their strength so depleted.

How far the shrewd Captain Robison's bluffing affected Langsdorff's plans is not known, but certainly it must have upset him to believe that the Admiralty had seen through his ruse.

Unhappily parted from his command, Captain Robison

could only watch and wait and hope that his signals had been picked up by some other ship which would relay them to British forces in the area. But the hours passed, and no sign of Allied warships became apparent to him, and he decided that his signals had failed to be detected. The transmitter was very weak, he knew all too well. Still, he had hoped …

In fact the *Newton Beech's* signals were picked up. The British steamer *Martand* had picked up part of a message, sufficient for them to know that the *Newton Beech* was being attacked by a German battleship, but for some reason her relay of the signal failed to secure any response.

Meanwhile the *Graf Spee* was sailing on to meet her third victim.

Chapter 4

Graf Spee's Third Victim

She was the *Ashlea*, owned by Clifford Shipping Co., Ltd., also of Newcastle-on-Tyne, 4,222 tons, bound from Durban to Freetown with a cargo of sugar.

Captain C. Pottinger first spotted the *Graf Spee* when she was ten miles away, off the port beam. This was October 7, over a week since the last news of the raider which had sunk the *Clement*, and at first he was not suspicious of her approach. She had the build of a French warship, and he thought she might in fact be the *Dunkerque*, so he kept steadily on his way and watched while the warship rapidly overhauled them. Because she was bow on, the *Ashlea* was unable to see what ensign she wore, if any, and it was only when she altered course and came broadside on that they saw the enormous German swastika streaming out over her stern. Then it was too late to do anything.

Simultaneously with the shock of seeing a mighty enemy warship right on top of them, they received a signal warning them not to use their radio or the German vessel would open fire. Another signal ordered them to heave to.

Captain Pottinger had no other course but to obey, but while giving his orders he ran below, taking the ship's confidential papers with him. Because the German warship was so close he was uneasy about throwing the documents overboard even in their special weighted bag, because he thought they might be recovered. Instead he made sure they were destroyed by personally thrusting them into the furnaces. When he returned to the bridge he found it already occupied by a German boarding party.

The German officer was not pleased, but merely ordered the *Ashlea*'s captain to get his men into the boats as they were going to destroy the vessel. This they did, sinking the ship with cartridge charges, while her crew were taken aboard the *Newton Beech*, which suddenly came up over the horizon.

Next day they sank the *Newton Beech*. She was too slow to accompany the battleship, so, no doubt reluctantly because it meant overcrowding the *Graf Spee*, Captain Langsdorff brought the British seamen across and sank the *Newton Beech* with further cartridge charges.

No signal had gone out from the *Ashlea* because of the speed of her capture, and back in London the Admiralty still waited for news of the South Atlantic raider. In any event they were waiting for news of the pocket battleship, the *Admiral Scheer*, not the *Graf Spee*. And they continued to have to wait, though again and again the German raider struck at British ships and sank or captured them.

Chapter 5

The S.S. Huntsman

Victim Number Four came within sight of the *Graf Spee's* keen look-outs in the evening of October 10, still in the waters between St. Helena and Ascension. She was a bigger ship than the first three captured by the German, a liner of 8,000 tons. Her name was the S.S. *Huntsman*, she belonged to the Harrison Line, and carried a crew of over eighty men. Her master was a Cheshire man, Captain A.H. Brown.

The officer of the watch reported to his captain about six in the evening that a man-o'-war was five miles to starboard and heading towards them fast. Captain Brown came up at once to inspect the oncomer, and after a few minutes also decided it was the French warship, the *Dunkerque*, because he knew the French were operating in the neighbourhood.

As the warship came speeding up, they saw a French flag at her stern, and that seemed to confirm Captain Brown's guess. However, suddenly, startlingly, when the ship was within a mile of them, they saw the French flag come down and in its place appear a mighty German swastika. Then it was too late to do much, though the captain at once ordered a radio message to be despatched.

And that was another radio message which never reached its target; it was an off-watch period for radio operators, and no one appeared to pick up the *Huntsman's* signal.

The merchantman was boarded by some very young but

very well-armed German sailors, whose commander ordered Captain Brown to follow the *Graf Spee*. Captain Langsdorff, it transpired, was in a dilemma. He had no room for a further eighty-odd prisoners aboard the *Graf Spee*, and he was not the kind of man to sink the *Huntsman* and turn her crew adrift in the middle of the vast Atlantic Ocean. It could be said of the German commander that he was a clean fighter and a humane opponent.

A few days later the crew of the *Huntsman* saw a third vessel on the horizon. Very soon they identified her as a German tanker, and guessed her to be a supply vessel for the *Graf Spee*. They were not to know then that the name of this German merchant ship was shortly to ring round the world, that its name was to be coupled with infamy, and that it was to provide the Royal Navy with yet another epic of courage and audacity.

It was the *Altmark*.

The *Huntsman* was plundered, the *Graf Spee* in turn serviced; then all the prisoners were taken aboard the *Altmark* and imprisoned below deck. Herded together in unclean and uncomfortable quarters, overcrowded and suffering because of inadequate ventilation, the British seamen for the first time really understood what it meant to be prisoners of war on the high seas. They were to have a long time to consider their condition.

The *Huntsman* was blown up when she had been robbed of all her oil and provisions, and then the *Graf Spee* and the *Altmark* parted. Captain Langsdorff had decided to move from the vicinity of the Ascension Island, because he rightly guessed that soon it would become a base for British ships searching for him. He knew that the hunt was intensifying for him, and he decided to leave the Atlantic for a while and try his luck in the Indian Ocean.

However, en route the battleship was to meet yet another victim, her fifth. At dawn, October 22, Captain Langsdorff ordered away his Arado seaplane to search for any enemy across their route. Within a short time the plane was back reporting the presence of a merchant ship almost directly ahead. Captain Langsdorff immediately altered course and went after her.

She was the S.S. *Trevanion*, 5,299 tons, Haim Shipping Company, Newcastle-on-Tyne, her master a Welshman from Barry, Captain J.W. Edwards.

The *Trevanion* wasn't taken easily. As soon as Captain Edwards identified the raider, he ordered his Radio Officer to transmit a raider signal. The *Graf Spee* immediately signalled, "Do not transmit or I will open fire." Captain Edwards promptly ordered, "Carry on with that signal."

Immediately the *Graf Spee* opened fire with her machine-guns from a range of about a hundred yards, spraying the *Trevanion*'s bridge and upper deck. The Radio Officer stopped transmitting, but Captain Edwards ran down to him and said, "Get that message out – all of it," and the transmission was resumed.

Once again the *Graf Spee* opened up with her machine-guns, and some of the bullets smashed their way into the Radio Room. Captain Edwards gave in only when he was told that all the message had gone out; he threw his secret papers overboard, then surrendered to the boarding party. An hour later the *Trevanion* was blown up and sunk, her crew prisoners aboard the *Graf Spee*.

No one had been hurt by the machine-gunning, remark-ably enough, and Captain Langsdorff could still proudly say to his prisoners that so far his efforts had not caused the loss of a single life. The British priosners of war (PoW) respected and even liked the German commander; he was ever courteous, always considerate, and in all ways treated them as he did the members of his crew.

Not so the commander of the *Altmark*, those prisoners aboard her were now discovering. Captain J.S. Dau was, by all accounts, a Nazi, seeming to hate the British seamen in his charge, and making little effort to alleviate their discomforts in the stifling quarters below deck. They prayed for rescue, for the Royal Navy to come up and give this Dau fellow what for, but the Navy was hunting blindly, without any clue as to the whereabouts of the raider since the *Clement's* call almost a month before.

The *Trevanion's* signal had failed to get through.

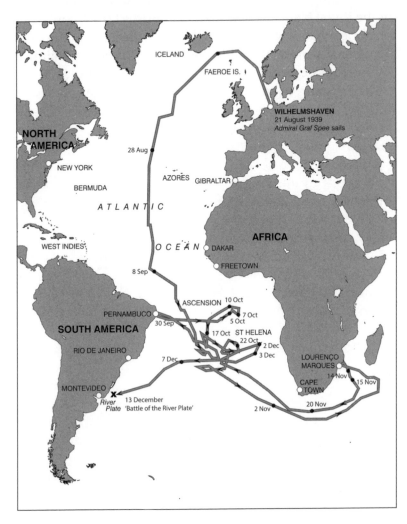

Above: The final cruise of the German heavy cruiser *Admiral Graf Spee*.

Chapter 6

The Tanker Africa Star

While the search for the *Graf Spee* went on in the Atlantic, with groups of cruisers and destroyers ceaselessly combing the vast ocean wastes, the pocket battleship slipped quietly round the southernmost tip of Africa and started to hunt in the Indian Ocean. Cruising parallel to the coast, out of sight of it but only about twenty miles off shore, Captain Langsdorff's search took him to a point off Lourenço Marques in Portuguese East Africa before he sighted his next victim.

She was a tiny ship, the *Africa Shell*, being no more than 706 tons; but she was a tanker, belonging to the Anglo-Saxon Petroleum Company, and her cargo in consequence was invaluable to the German raider.

Captain F.G. Dove, master of the *Africa Shell*, spotted the oncoming battleship shortly after midday. She was flying French colours, and for a while, like other skippers before him, he thought she was a Frenchman. Then suddenly he became suspicious, and in his own words, "I ran for it." The huge battleship found herself having to chase the tiniest victim so far encountered.

It became a race for the shore, with the *Africa Shell* doing its damnedest to get into the safety of neutral waters – and succeeding, too. They were well inside neutral territory when the German opened fire with one of his 5.9-inch guns. The shell fell astern, but Captain Dove knew there was no escape, and the next salvo would for certain blow them out of the water.

He threw his papers over the side, took bearings and found himself only two miles off-shore. When Captain Langsdorff brought him aboard the *Graf Spee* he made his protest, but it did him no good. The *Africa Shell* was looted, then sunk ...

Still the world was unaware of the raider's depredations, because yet another ship had not been able to transmit a warning ... for the *Africa Shell* carried no radio.

But though Captain Dove had been taken prisoner aboard the German battleship, to everyone's surprise Captain Langsdorff made no attempt to prevent the crew of the British tanker from rowing to the shore. They had only two miles to go, and within hours they were ashore and their story was being flashed to the ends of the earth.

A battleship raider was out again. The pocket battleship had struck in the Indian Ocean, and now the field of search had been widened into two oceans – two oceans to comb for an elusive enemy, at a time when the demands of war were an intolerable burden upon a Navy still virtually at peace-time strength only. The odds, if momentarily, were certainly in favour of Hitler's lone marauder.

The odds lengthened that night, because immediately Captain Langsdorff had allowed his presence to become known in the Indian Ocean, he turned south and sped as fast as he could into the Atlantic again. Keep 'em guessing, was Langsdorff's motto during those weeks, and he certainly had his searchers guessing by the speed of his manœuvres.

Chapter 7

The Liner Doric Star

The next victim *did* get away a distress signal, and it was picked up and relayed to the British naval radio station at Simonstown. She was the *Doric Star*, seventh victim to fall to the raider and the first in two months to radio the information to the waiting hunting groups in the southern hemisphere.

The *Doric Star* was a magnificent prize, a Blue Star cargo liner of over 10,000 tons, carrying butter, cheese and frozen meat from New Zealand and Australia to the UK. The *Graf Spee* was cruising in her old hunting grounds near St. Helena in the mid-Atlantic when, about noon on December 2, her scouting aircraft reported smoke on the horizon. The *Graf Spee*, which had refuelled from the *Altmark* only a few days earlier, closed in fast on the biggest prize she had encountered so far. The raider, incidentally, was in disguise, having rigged up a dummy funnel aft of the forward turret and another forward, and with other alterations was now able to pass, at least from some distance away, as the British battle cruiser, the *Renown*.

The attack on the *Doric Star* represented a departure from the usual tactics so successfully employed to date by Captain Langsdorff, and speculation might be made as to the reason for it. In attacking previous victims, Langsdorff had exerted guile to get his ship so close to his prey that it had little chance to radio off a warning of his approach.

But when his pilot reported the presence of the *Doric Star*, Langsdorff opened fire on the Blue Star vessel when he was about fifteen miles away, giving the British ship ample time to transmit a raider warning. The curious, inexplicable change of tactics was eventually to bring the *Graf Spee* to battle, and be the cause of the death of her commander. What makes the long-range attack the more remarkable is that in his guise as a British warship, it should have been easy for him to have come to close range with the British cargo liner without alarming his victim, just as on previous occasions.

But Langsdorff opened fire, and a startled British crew saw a shell burst quite near to them. Immediately they looked round for the vessel that was gunning them, but the ocean seemed deserted save for themselves. It was astonishing.

Then someone propounded a theory, "It must be a submarine," and everyone started to look for a conning-tower. But there wasn't one in sight. Minutes later, while still perplexed, the look-out sighted the mast of the *Graf Spee* over the horizon, and immediately mistook it for a submarine periscope. In time, though, it became all too apparent that a German warship was their assailant, but even before this the master of the *Doric Star*, Captain W. Stubbs, had ordered his Radio Officer, Mr. William Comber, to transmit a raider report as fast as possible. For once a victim had the time to transmit a warning, and the remarkable thing is that Captain Langsdorff should have varied his tactics so that such an eventuality was possible.

Comber got to work, but aboard the *Graf Spee* they began to jam him with a radio set taken from the *Newton Beech*, and this presented problems in transmission. Langsdorff was informed of the *Doric Star's* impudence, which continued even after she was signalled to cease transmitting, so the *Graf Spee's* captain again ordered his gun to fire. A solitary round was despatched from a 3.7. The shot fell short, and the *Graf Spee* radio operators reported that the *Doric Star's* transmission had ceased.

The cargo ship was drifting to a halt now, her crew swinging out her lifeboats and preparing to abandon ship. The *Graf Spee* came gliding up majestically to take over her prize.

Suddenly, dramatically, again the *Doric Star's* radio began to tap out the raider report. Radio Officer Comber had not yet surrendered. Before the *Graf Spee* could jam the report, a vital part of it had gone out, to be picked up by some other ship and re-transmitted again. But this Langsdorff did not know at the time, neither did he know it was the first link in a chain that was to bring his ship to battle and help to write British naval history.

Langsdorff wanted this prize. The *Star* was comparatively new, one of the finest cargo ships afloat. She would be as valuable to the raider as the *Altmark,* heading for the next rendezvous with the pocket battleship. A prize crew went away and boarded the *Doric Star,* but almost immediately signalled a message that shattered Langsdorff's fine plans for using the vessel. "Engines deliberately sabotaged by *Doric Star's* Chief Engineer." The Chief had anticipated Langsdorff's intentions and had, literally, decided to throw a spanner in the works. Regretfully, he had to order her to be sunk.

In another way Langsdorff was cheated. The *Doric Star's* cargo of meat, butter and cheese would have been a welcome change to the diet of the German sailors, but when Captain Stubbs was asked, "What cargo are you carrying?" he answered, "Wool." As luck would have it, some bales of wool were on top of the foodstuffs and when several hatches were opened and only wool was discovered, the Germans lost interest and made no further search of the ship.

Captain Langsdorff was worried by the report that some part of the *Doric Star's* signal might have got through, and he waited anxiously while his operators listened to signals from other stations.

Two hours later, just when he was congratulating himself that their kill had gone unnoticed, a signal came up from the radio room. Someone was transmitting a relay of the *Doric Star*'s message. The secret of his presence – the precise position of his ship – was being broadcast to the world.

It was time the *Graf Spee* got away from those waters, grave of five victims of the raider.

While he was still planning his next move, two signals were brought to him in quick succession. The first told of an intercepted signal from a British warship, now relaying the *Doric Star*'s raider report and position; the second said that Simonstown radio had picked it up and was flashing the news to the Admiralty in Whitehall. The hunt was beginning.

Captain Langsdorff decided to head towards the coast of South America, well away from the Cape to Freetown trade route which he had been harrying, and away went his ship as fast as she could clear the now dangerous waters. Langsdorff was still trying to out-bluff his enemies, and he felt that the coast near to where he had made his first kill would be the last place to be considered as his new haunt by the British Navy. By now he considered that his strategy in the Indian Ocean would have caused substantial naval forces to be withdrawn from the South Atlantic trade routes, and still further units of the British Navy would be hurrying towards the scene of his latest kill, the St. Helena area.

With little real concern, then – much more concerned to be able to make rendezvous with the *Altmark* when the fuel position began to be critical – Captain Lansgdorff headed the *Graf Spee* into waters which he felt would be clear of his enemies.

Chapter 8
Tairoa

A few hours later, at dawn on December 3, they found themselves running on to another big cargo ship, and Captain Langsdorff could not resist the chance to take a further prize.

The ship was the *Tairoa*, nearly 8,000 tons, of the Furness, Withy Line, her master, Captain W.B.S. Starr, of Liverpool. Captain Starr had heard the raider report from the unfortunate *Doric Star* the previous day, and had swung westward to avoid the danger area. It was an unhappy decision, in the light of subsequent events, because the raider, too, had turned west and so had run on to them.

Not knowing what had sunk the *Doric Star*, whether submarine, armed merchant cruiser, or battleship, only knowing that she had been attacked, Captain Starr was uneasy and on the bridge before dawn. So it was that with first light he saw the faint smoke of the raider on the port bow.

Captain Starr could not positively identify the oncoming battleship as hostile while at a distance, so he hesitated about sending out an S.O.S. signal. Then he saw a French flag on the warship, and began to feel reassured. All the same, he watched the raider closely, ready to take action at any untoward behaviour, his lifeboats cleared and ready for lowering.

Suddenly the crew of the *Tairoa* saw a new ensign going up on the warship, and they gasped when they saw it unfurl into a mighty swastika flag. They had been tricked, and now the raider was only two miles away and her mighty guns were trained straight upon them. Captain Starr saw a signal – "Stop your engines," and a shell exploded in the sea near to them to show that the raided meant business.

Captain Starr immediately ordered his radio operator to send a signal: "*Attacked by German battleship* Admiral Scheer" – together with their position.

Aboard the *Graf Spee*, they immediately detected the use of the transmitter, and at once the battleship opened fire to stop the signal. Shells smashed the bridge, officers' quarters and radio room, and the steering gear was put out of action.

Before the radio room was wrecked, however, the operator, Mr. P.J. Cummins, twice managed to get the signal away, and was still transmitting, lying on the deck, when shell splinters demolished his apparatus. For this courageous act he was later awarded the M.B.E. Much more important, the signal did not go out undetected, and within hours the ether was humming with the news that again the raider had struck and another ship had been captured.

The *Admiral Scheer*, of course. By now it appeared to have been established that two pocket battleships were operating, the *Admiral Scheer* in the Atlantic (on the report of the crew of the *Clement*), and the *Graf Spee* in the Indian Ocean ... because of the report of the crew of the *Africa Shell*. Captain Langsdorff's bluff had, after all, been successful.

Again Captain Langsdorff decided to keep the big cargo ship as tender to the *Graf Spee*, and again he was disappointed. The ship was found to be useless because of her damaged steering gear, and so Langsdorff ordered her to be sunk. The *Tairoa*'s crew of eighty-one were brought aboard the battleship, already uncomfortably crowded with prisoners from the earlier raid, and then she was torpedoed.

Immediately the unfortunate *Tairoa* had gone under the Atlantic, Langsdorff ordered a course west and headed towards the busy River Plate area, two thousand miles away. He had all the mighty ocean to choose from; he could have sailed north, south, east or west, a tiny speck upon a vast ocean, and he picked upon the one place where he felt sure he could continue to make his kills and yet be far away from an enemy.

Yet two thousand miles away a British naval officer put his finger on the map and said, "That's where she'll turn up next." He called her the *Admiral Scheer*, true, but his finger rested on the River Plate area. Confidently he even predicted the exact time when she would reach the area, and gave orders for his ships to go out and meet the enemy.

He was Commodore Henry Harwood Harwood, O.B.E., Commanding South America Division of the America and West Indies Squadron.

Chapter 9

H.M.S. Exeter Sighted

It was not guesswork on the part of Commodore Harwood that made him place the next operations area of the pocket battleship off the River Plate. To him it seemed logical that a raider would want to get astride a busy sea route, and now that the Cape to Freetown lane had become "hot" he reasoned that the pocket battleship would be quickly moving on to another area.

The question was, which one? Commodore Harwood decided on the Plate because in those waters sailed the rich cargoes from South America, vital to Britain's war-time needs, especially of grain and meat.

Commodore Harwood (then Captain H.H. Harwood, O.B.E.) had been appointed to the South America Division in August, 1937. During the absence through illness of Vice-Admiral S.J. Meyrick, C.B., Harwood took command, his flagship being H.M.S. *Exeter*.

Commodore Harwood had specialised in torpedoes during the First World War, serving aboard the cruiser *Sutlej* and the battleship *Royal Sovereign*. For four years from 1922 he served at the Admiralty in the Plans Division, after which he was in command of H.M.S. *London* as Flag Captain in the First Cruiser Squadron. After that came two years on the training staff of the Royal Naval College, and thence his transfer to the South America Division.

Harwood was a fluent Spanish linguist, and by all accounts did much to make friends for Britain in South America by his social activities. British standing was high, which proved to be fortunate for us during the war years, especially in Uruguay and Chile, where the two British cruisers, *Exeter* and *Ajax*, had performed magnificent rescue work following the earthquake at Concepcion.

Harwood's command formed one of the hunting groups allocated the task of seeking out and destroying the pocket battleship raider, and it is interesting to see how seemingly hopeless were their chances in this direction.

Four cruisers comprised Harwood's hunting group – the *Exeter* (Captain F.S. Bell), *Cumberland* (Captain W.H.G. Fallowfield), *Achilles* (Captain W.E. Parry), and *Ajax* (Captain C.H.L. Woodhouse). Four ... but rarely had Commodore Harwood more than three ships available because of the problems of refuelling off a neutral coast during war-time.

By the accepted terms of neutrality, no country would permit a belligerent warship to refuel more than once in three months in their waters. For the South America Division this meant the use of the Falkland Islands in the South Atlantic for refuelling as well as refitting, almost 1,900 miles from Rio de Janeiro, and a thousand miles from Montevideo. Always, it seemed, one of his cruisers was having to journey south for refuelling, so that with three cruisers only he was left to police the long South American coast and search at the same time for the mysterious pocket battleship, the supposed *Admiral Scheer*.

It was, of course, too much to expect that such a little force could be able to keep effective watch over three thousand miles of coastline as well as the vast sea area off South America. All Commodore Harwood could hope to do was make sporadic appearances off the South American ports, causing German shipping to be detained long enough to warrant internment. In this regard Britain was considerably assisted by reports from agents and friends of the U.K. in all the South American countries, who supplied useful information about German shipping in ports there.

Not that all reports seemed helpful at the time. As an example, on September 8, Harwood received a signal from the Admiralty informing him that three German ships, the *General Artigas*, *Monte Pascoal* and *Gloria*, were assembling off the southernmost point of South America, off the coast of Patagonia. The report indicated a possibility of the ships picking up German reservists in South American countries, notably Argentina, with a view to attacking and taking possession of the Falkland Islands. *Ajax* was immediately sent off to counter the move.

Less than forty-eight hours later a second signal threw doubt upon the accuracy of the first. Now it was considered by agents in South America that German reservists did not constitute a danger, and the threat potential in the three Nazi raiders might be somewhat discounted.

So *Ajax* was recalled.

Almost immediately came a third signal. The scare was still on. German reservists *were* concentrating in South American ports. They could have but one objective, it was repeated, an attack on the Falkland Islands, at the moment undefended save for a few small shore guns.

Ajax must start her long dash to the Falklands, after all.

Life could be hell for a British commodore with too many demands placed upon a force quite inadequate for the magnitude of the task expected of it. But as this is a general condition in the Royal Navy, at any rate in time of war, Commodore Harwood probably said a few sailorly things and got on with the job.

Ajax, incidentally, that much-travelled cruiser, had the distinction of being the first British ship to sink an enemy in World War II. On September 3, 1939, at 1330, only three hours after the declaration of war upon Germany, she sighted a merchant ship which proved to be German. She was the S.S. *Olinda*, bound from Montevideo to Germany with a cargo of wool, hides, cotton and scrap iron.

Circumstances were against the *Ajax* putting a prize crew aboard, so the *Olinda's* crew were taken off and the ship sunk.

As if that was not enough, the following day the *Ajax* chased another German merchantman and sank her. This time it was the 7,000-ton *Carl Fritzen*. Captain Woodhouse was in a hurry to get on with the war.

Woodhouse served in the First World War as a sub-lieutenant and lieutenant in H.M.S. *Bristol*. He was promoted to Commander in 1927 and Captain in 1934 ... appointed to command *Ajax* in 1937.

Of interest is the fact that with H.M.S. *Bristol* he was in action in the Battle of the Falkland Islands against the German China Squadron under the command of Admiral Graf von Spee. Hitler named the third and latest of his pocket battleships after von Spee, who had become an almost legendary hero to his countrymen.

Admiral von Spee, a German count, had won a decisive battle over a British squadron commanded by Admiral Cradock on November 1, 1914, off the seaport of Coronel in Chile. In this the *Monmouth* and *Good Hope* had been sunk, with many lives lost before the action was broken off by the British. It was Britain's usual bad beginning to a war, but such a defeat at sea had shocked the nation while sending Germany into an ecstasy of delight.

On December 8, 1914, however, the situation was dramatically reversed when a British squadron under Admiral Sturdee caught the Germans off the Falkland Islands and destroyed them, von Spee going down with his ship and being drowned.

Captain Woodhouse, then, had a long-standing experience of war in South Atlantic waters and in the first months of World War II had quite a bag of enemy prizes to his credit.

Soon he was to take part in another resounding victory in southern waters.

Quite unaware of Harwood's brilliant deduction, Captain Langsdorff was heading for the busy River Plate area. On the way, though, he paused long enough to make yet another quiet kill.

Harwood, incidentally, had transferred his flag from the *Exeter* to the *Ajax* shortly before this, and was aboard the smaller cruiser as the *Graf Spee* came at leisure across the sunny waters of the warm South Atlantic towards the killing ground.

The *Graf Spee* had rendezvoused in mid-Atlantic with the soon-to-be-notorious *Altmark* on December 6, put aboard her most of the crews of the *Tairoa* and *Doric Star*, and taken in further provisions and fuel. They had parted, arranging a rendezvous in a few days' time in the River Plate area, preparatory to both making a dash for Germany, for by now the *Graf Spee* had been continuously at sea since the middle of August and was in need of overhaul.

Leaving the slower *Altmark* behind, Langsdorff had hurried north-west to make a few further quick kills before the long and hazardous journey into the colder waters around his native Europe. For another day he kept on his course until he knew he was close to the trade routes to the South American ports, and now, with impatience, he waited for his ninth prize to come along.

While he was waiting he received signals from Berlin which told him of British warship movements in the Southern Hemisphere. *Ajax, Achilles, Exeter* and *Cumberland* were along the South American coast, the *Renown* and *Ark Royal*, among other ships, were concentrating on West Africa, with the cruisers *Sussex* and *Shropshire* at Cape Town and Simonstown. Germany had many friends diligently reporting for her in Africa and America.

Early on the evening of December 7, smoke was sighted by the vigilant look-out in the *Graf Spee*. They altered course and bore down upon the ship which quickly resolved into a merchantman – a small ship, but if British worthy of destruction.

It was British, ninth victim to fall to the raider. She was the *Streonshalh*, 3,895 tons, of the Marwood Steamship Company of Whitby. Her cargo was wheat, consigned from Rosario to the U.K. Ministry of Food, her crew numbered thirty-two, and her master was Captain J.R. Robinson.

Captain Robinson was reading on the lower bridge. About 1800 the Chief Officer came down from the bridge and said, "I think there's a sailing ship on the horizon."

A sailing ship! That was interesting. Captain Robinson immediately went to the top bridge and got out his telescope. By now the ship was nearer, and the captain exclaimed, "That's no sailing ship. It's the fighting top of a cruiser."

He lowered the telescope and did some hard thinking. He had heard the *Doric Star's* distress signal a few days earlier, and knew there was a German raider in the vicinity. But this might not be a raider, it might be a British cruiser. There was no sense in sending out S.O.S.s if the ship turned out to be friendly, and he had a feeling it was British.

All the same, he ordered the ship's lifeboats to be provisioned and swung out ready to be lowered, then he turned his telescope upon the oncoming battleship. She kept on approaching, bows on all the time, so that he could not read the signals she was flying – which was as Langsdorff intended it. She was moving in at high speed, too, and Captain Robinson grew more and more uneasy.

But suddenly, abruptly, when close up to the *Streonshalh*, the pocket battleship changed course, and at once Captain Robinson saw the flag she was flying at her stern – the biggest Nazi flag he had ever seen. At the same time they were able to see signals, and one read: "If you transmit on your radio I will open fire immediately."

The range was point-blank; there was nothing Captain Robinson could do but obey the peremptory command of the German. His radio was silent, but in other ways he was active.

He hurled the ship's papers overboard in the weighted bag supplied to all merchantmen at the beginning of hostilities, halted the ship and ordered his boats away. However, the crew were not allowed to row for the very distant shore this time, as in the case of the *Africa Shell*'s men, but were ordered across to the raider. They came unwillingly, sullen at being taken prisoner so unexpectedly.

A boarding party came up and were met by a grim-faced Captain Robinson, a twice-torpedoed veteran of the First World War. The ship was ransacked, and some booty carried across to the battleship, slowly circling round the motionless British merchantman. Then Captain Robinson was taken across, and to his surprise (but doubtless some pleasure) found other of his countrymen already aboard. He was told they were being well-treated – as well as could be expected in the circumstances – and was relieved to learn that their captor appeared to be a most gentlemanly pirate. He was given a meal of black bread and margarine and some coffee, then later a glass of beer.

The *Streonshalh* was sunk by bombs placed in each of her four holds, and then the *Graf Spee* began to glide away from the graveyard of her latest victim.

Five months at sea, tens of thousands of miles traversed – nine British victims totalling 50,089 tons, and not one single life lost. The prisoners aboard the speeding *Graf Spee* realised that their German captor took pride in his record, especially in being able to boast that no one had died as a result of his activities. The prisoners knew they were lucky to have fallen into such good hands – how lucky only the unfortunates sweating in their misery in the hell-ship *Altmark* knew. Any one of them would have given anything in the world to be back with the courteous, fair-dealing Captain Langsdorff, instead of suffering in a ship never designed to carry such large numbers of men. But no one could change their situation. Prisoners they were, and prisoners they would remain for many more thousands of miles, right until they were on the doorstep of Germany. . . .

A few minutes after dawn on December 13, the *Graf Spee* sighted the tall masts of yet another ship. Action Stations were sounded, and her crew took post, while the powerful pocket battleship leapt into top speed, racing in for one more kill. Then a call came down from the lookout, and it was urgent, filled with a quality not heard before.

The ship ahead was no unarmed and helpless merchant-man. It was a ship of war, a cruiser.

And those distinctive tall masts told them it was the British man-o'-war, the *Exeter*.

Chapter 10

The River Plate

Commodore Harwood had made his decision. "She will cruise at about 15 knots," Commodore Harwood had concluded, "and that will bring her to the Rio de Janeiro focal area in the morning of December 12, off the River Plate in the afternoon of the same day, and the Falkland Islands on December 14th." That is, if the pocket battleship stayed in the Atlantic, intending to harry our sea lanes.

Which area should he decide on? That was the question. Yet unhesitatingly Commodore Harwood said, "The River Plate," and immediately ordered his hunting group to prepare for a rendezvous with the raider.

As events turned out, Commodore Harwood had only three ships at his disposal, and for the moment they were widely dispersed. At the time of the news of the attack on the *Doric Star*, *Ajax* was at Port Stanley with *Exeter*, both cruisers indulging in a much needed rest and self-refit. *Achilles* was in the Rio de Janeiro area, and the *Cumberland* in the River Plate. No other naval forces were near enough to take effective part in Commodore Harwood's plans when he decided that the pocket battleship might next be expected to turn up off the River Plate.

Cumberland, an eight 8-inch gun cruiser, was badly in need of a refit, and Commodore Harwood ordered her immediately to the Falklands for a self-refit, but told Captain Fallowfield to be in a state of readiness, prepared to move at short notice on two shafts.

He ordered the *Ajax* to sea immediately, the *Exeter* to follow after completion of repairs on December 8. *Achilles* was ordered to Montevideo to refuel, also to leave on December 8, all three cruisers to concentrate in the River Plate area on December 12. Strict W/T silence was maintained after Commodore Harwood's signal was flashed out; unusual radio activity must not scare away the approaching pocket battleship.

Harwood had three ships to the enemy's one, but in only one other respect had he the advantage. His largest cruiser was still small compared with the pocket battleships, completely out of date in design, as demonstrated by Admiral Raeder's new vessels, and only slightly faster.

The *Exeter*, West-country named and almost entirely West-country manned, had been laid down in 1928 and completed in 1931. She could be described as orthodox in construction and in naval circles that could be construed as criticism in itself. Certainly the pocket battleships could not be described in any way as orthodox.

Against the pocket battleships' true displacement of approaching 13,000 tons, the Exeter was only 8,390 tons – *Ajax* and *Achilles* were much smaller with a displacement of 6,985 tons. *Exeter* carried six 8-inch guns in three double turrets, four 4-inch anti-aircraft guns and six torpedo tubes. Her speed was thirty-two knots.

The pocket battleship's 11-inch guns could throw a projectile weighing 670 pounds a distance of 30,000 yards, against *Exeter's* range of about 27,000 yards, for her biggest shell weighing only 256 pounds ... *Exeter*, in fact, could be out-ranged by about two miles, but even this was not the most significant factor in any possible battle.

The German battleships were massively armoured, protected by four-inch steel in vital areas, with internal armour 1½ inches thick; on her gun turrets was seven-inch plating. If the *Exeter*'s shells landed on the pocket battleships, except at very close range it was not expected that they would penetrate the enemy armour and do any damage. But all knew, and later events were to prove it, that one 11-inch shell landing on the thinly-armoured cruiser could virtually put the ship out of action.

On paper, with superior armament and massively armoured, the battleships could be contemptuous of any opposition from the smaller *Exeter*. What chance, then, had the much smaller cruisers, *Ajax* and *Achilles*, against a modern pocket battleship.

Ajax, laid down in 1933, completed in 1935; main armament eight 6-inch guns mounted in four double turrets, eight 4-inch anti-aircraft guns, eight torpedo tubes. *Achilles*, laid down in 1931, completed in 1933, with the same armament as *Ajax*.

Ajax and *Achilles* with their thin skin of armour to protect them against 670-pound shells, only able to hurl 100-pound projectiles in reply, and outranged by over three miles. The theorists of warfare, certainly in Germany, would have said that the three British cruisers were heading to their death when they sailed to intercept the supposed *Admiral Scheer*: the pocket battleship would sink them all in turn before they came close enough with their guns to hurt the German raider.

Experts are notoriously wrong, though in this case they should have been right. Even the fact that all three smaller cruisers were faster than the battleship seemed no advantage; for speed seemed only likely to bring them more quickly into range of projectiles, any one of which could sink them.

Two factors were on the British side, however, still important even in an era of armour-plate and 11-inch guns. British seamanship and guts.

Chapter 11
Dawn, 13 December 1939

HMS *Achilles* had been appointed to the South America Division on October 27, 1939. She was under the command of Captain W.E. Parry, who joined the Navy in 1905 and passed out head of his term of cadets at Dartmouth, gaining five firsts in his Lieutenant tests.

He was a torpedo specialist, and served with the *Birmingham* in the Grand Fleet during World War I. Later, he was Executive Officer of the aircraft-carrier *Eagle* in China, was Commander of the Anti-Submarine Establishment at Portland, then at the Imperial Defence College, finally joining *Achilles* in 1938.

Achilles had been lent to the New Zealand Government as a training ship for New Zealand ratings, and was in Auckland at the outbreak of war. Her crew consisted of 327 New Zealanders, a few of whom were Maoris. Captain Parry was quick to notice the absence of racial prejudice in the New Zealanders, and how almost fanatically proud they were of their Maori comrades. It was a fine ship, with a well-trained and disciplined crew, and Commodore Harwood welcomed it when he received news of her appointment to his Division.

When ordered to meet *Ajax* and *Exeter* in the River Plate, *Achilles* was patrolling off Pernambuco and Cabadello, to the annoyance of German shipping trapped therein and not daring to venture out. The Brazilian Air Force had come out to investigate the appearance of a warship off her coast, and added much to everyone's confusion by identifying the *Achilles* as a pocket battleship. This did not help an over-taxed British Admiralty, but in time Captain Parry was able to reassure them.

Sailing south, *Achilles* called in at Montevideo to refuel, where she received a wonderful reception from the Uruguayans, friendly towards the British cause and only too anxious to demonstrate their feelings.

Ajax, meanwhile, was hastening to join *Achilles* and *Exeter* in the River Plate area. On December 5 she received a signal from the British Naval Attaché at Buenos Aires that the *Ussukuma*, a 7,800-ton German steamer, had left Bahia Blanca at 1900 on December 4. Harwood promptly ordered the *Ajax* at speed towards Montevideo, guessing that the German merchant ship would try to reach the port inside territorial waters.

The anticipation proved excellent, and was an augury of success for his prophecies anent the pocket battleship (as Commodore Harwood still thought), the *Admiral Scheer*.

At 1910 on December 5, smoke was sighted from a steamer on the horizon, course was altered and the *Ajax* closed in. It was the *Ussukuma*. Captain Woodhouse ordered her to heave to, and sent a boarding party across, but the crew of the *Ussukuma* had had ample time and scuttled their ship. *Ajax* then went on to join *Achilles*, a couple of hundred miles east of Montevideo. Two days later *Exeter* joined them.

Now the hunting group was ready. The *Ussukuma* had been merely an incident, routine in the affairs of the *Ajax*. The next hours and days would be of greater interest.

Commodore Harwood then took his ships to a position 32° south, 47° west, the position chosen by him for their meeting with the German raider. It was a congested area with many shipping lanes converging on the estuary, the kind of situation exactly made to suit a surface raider.

At 1200, December 12, Commodore Harwood signalled his

battle orders to his captains. They were brief, concise and beyond ambiguity.

My policy, his signal said, *with three cruisers in company versus one pocket battleship. Attack at once by day or night.*

The traditional approach by the Royal Navy ... attack.

By day act as two units. 1st Division (Ajax *and* Achilles) *and* Exeter *diverged to permit flank marking. First Division will concentrate gunfire. By night ships will normally remain in company in open order.*

That day the three ships practised the manœuvre of working as two divisions, carrying out concentration and marking exercises. When that was done, came the testing time of waiting to see if the commanding officer's calculations would prove right.

Perhaps for Commodore Harwood it was an anxious time, but if so he did not show it. And yet he must have doubted his own prophecies: it seemed too much to imagine that with dawn the following morning the picture would be just as he had prophesied it, with the elusive, much-sought-after German battleship obligingly coming over the horizon right into their arms. Far too much to expect.

Dawn, December 13, 1939. First a little light and nothing much to be seen except the unusually calm waters of the South Atlantic. The crews were at Dawn Action Stations. Then more light as the sun came lifting to the rim of the horizon – *Achilles* and *Exeter*, long grey shapes low in the water, became discernible. They began to form up in battle order, and still the light strengthened. They were proceeding at 14 knots on a course of 060, *Ajax* leading, *Achilles* astern of her, and *Exeter* a mile to the rear.

Ajax spotted the smoke first, an almost insignificant scar on the horizon on the port beam. The time was 0609. Captain Woodhouse reported it to Commodore Harwood, who had just gone below.

"Signal the *Exeter* to close in and investigate," ordered Harwood, and came up on deck again.

The *Exeter* acknowledged receipt of the signal, and Captain Bell pulled out of line and went hurrying north towards the smoke cloud. Captain Bell, but recently promoted in 1938; midshipman in the cruisers *Cumberland* and *Challenger*; later in the *Canada* during the first World War … much later commander of the battle cruiser *Renown* … Captain Bell listened to the speculation around him about the distant plume of smoke but reserved his own opinion.

Almost at once someone declared he could make out a pocket battleship, but general opinion for a minute or two was that it was a merchantman. Then, quite suddenly, the smoke seemed to lift and they were able to see more clearly.

They saw the fighting top of a warship.

At once the alarm rattlers sounded, while a signal was despatched to Commodore Harwood – *I think it is a pocket battleship.*

Instantly the mood induced by routine and monotony fled from the British cruiser. Throughout the ship surged the excitement, the mounting thrill that always precedes battle. Here was the elusive German raider, the ship they had hunted for two and a half months. She was within sight, and they had the speed on her and she couldn't run away from them this time. Nobody cheered, but it was a nerve-tingling moment; for all knew that this was to be the first naval battle of the Second World War, and they were to participate in it.

Commodore Harwood's plan of battle, rehearsed the previous evening, now came into instant operation. The squadron immediately formed into two divisions, 1st Division, *Ajax* and *Achilles*, 2nd Division, *Exeter* – in other words, the smaller cruisers would hunt and fight together, while *Exeter* operated alone.

Exeter turned northwest, while the other two cruisers sped as fast as their accelerating engines would take them on a diverging course north-east. The pocket battleship would thus come between the two divisions and be forced to engage both simultaneously, thereby reducing her concentration of fire.

The pocket battleship could be seen, racing in at high speed, not seeking to avoid battle. Only two minutes after Captain Bell had sent his signal to Commodore Harwood the German warship opened fire upon *Exeter* with her main armament. Two minutes later, at 0620, *Exeter* opened up with her 8-inch guns.

And still the German battleship came on, and that, considering Captain Langsdorff's orders from Berlin, was astonishing.

Chapter 12

The Graf Spee Could no Longer Avoid Battle

The role of a German surface raider was to be a nuisance to the enemy and to cause a disproportionately large naval force to be tied up in an effort to nullify its activities. It was to hurt without risk of harm to herself, to attack helpless merchantmen and not engage any enemy, even weaker than the *Graf Spee*, if there was the slightest danger of sustaining damage to the ship. Captain Langsdorff's orders were, quite positively, to run away and not fight any Allied warships or even well-armed merchantmen; and this was not a policy of cowardice but sound naval tactics, calculated to serve Germany's ends better than one encouraging naval battles.

Germany's war fleet was too small to risk damage to any unit of it; and even slight injury in the course of a successful battle could be disastrous to a pocket battleship cruising so far from home.

That, in fact, was the problem – the thousands of miles between the raider and the well-equipped naval yards of Germany where major repairs could be effected. For the British, with ports all over the world, some damage could always be repaired in reasonable time, and the vessel be soon back on patrol on the high seas. But if the *Graf Spee* were to sustain some injury – say, a hole below the water-line or damage to her engines – even though she won her battle and got away safely, it would indeed be disastrous.

For if the damage could not be repaired by her crew at sea, it would mean she would have to run the gauntlet of the well-guarded North Atlantic approaches to Europe, cruising far north in an effort to slip unobserved down the North Sea to Germany, a distance of perhaps twelve thousand miles – a long way to go for a repair and a long time to be out of action.

Langsdorff's orders were beyond ambiguity, yet on the morning of December 13, when he saw the tall masts of the *Exeter*, for a full fifteen minutes he kept the *Graf Spee* on a course heading straight towards the British warship.

Why? It is a question which was asked by the British commodore and captains, by Raeder and Hitler in Berlin when they got to know, and for years later by naval strategists the world over.

"Keep out of trouble," Langsdorff had been ordered, as all German captains of surface raiders had been told. Yet deliberately, this fateful day of December 13, 1939, he sought combat with a British warship. And if that wasn't asking for trouble, nothing was.

"Run for it rather than risk being hurt," they had told him. And they had equipped him with radar to give him vision over his opponents. This day it was proving troublesome again, and gave him no warning of what was over the horizon, but all the same there is no doubt that his look-outs, from the superior heights where they maintained unceasing watch, spotted the *Exeter* before the British cruisers saw that troublesome smoke from the German. Langsdorff had "time to turn aside and space to flee," to slip inconspicuously into the vastness of the sea around him, if he had wanted, for the enemy was without that long-seeing radar to help them.

If Langsdorff had done that, if he had ordered his ship to run for it, unobserved, there would have been no terrible naval action that day, no dramatic end, beyond the prophecy of all who saw the beginning of the fight, to one of the world's finest battleships. And there would have been no personal tragedy, so far as Langsdorff was concerned – a tragedy, blazoned in the largest-sized type from most newspapers in the world, sufficient to shock even Germany's enemies.

Harwood would have been left waiting for a ship which would never have come. After hours or days he would have been discredited as a prophet, never knowing how completely accurate his forecast had been. In which event, perhaps the honours which rightly came to him might never have been his, and yet he would have been just as deserving of them. Upon such slender chances, the inexplicable conduct of another, does fame or comparative obscurity depend.

True, there are reports that Langsdorff's look-outs made a mistake over the masts of the *Exeter*. His information from Berlin, presumably via South America, had indicated the sailing of a particularly valuable prize, the *Highland Monarch*, a 14,000-ton Royal Mail Line ship, from the River Plate. There appears to have been an assumption that it would be in convoy, and when the *Exeter*'s were sighted they might have been taken for those of destroyer.

A destroyer. No match for a mighty battleship. Perhaps Langsdorff had visions of sweeping in and blowing the tiny warship right out of the water with one murderous salvo from his big guns, and then running amok amid a helpless convoy, truly a wolf among toothless sheep. True, Langsdorff had been told to take not the slightest risk, and going for a British warship, however small, inevitably involved the possibility of some damage.

But perhaps Langsdorff was tired of running away and weary of doing no better than chasing lumbering merchant-men, like frightened old ladies, to their destruction. He was bred to a fighting trade, and perhaps in a mood of reck-lessness he could not resist an engagement with the tradi-tional enemies of his country.

He was going home very shortly, anyway, and this might have been an influencing factor. He might have argued,

"What if I do get hurt?" A little ship like a destroyer, he might have argued, could not vitally affect his prospects of returning home, and if he needed repairs beyond those possible at sea, they would soon put them to rights in Germany.

Probably, too, the thought of winding up his voyage in a blaze of glory proved irresistible to him. Never before had a powerful battleship been given such an opportunity for hurting enemy shipping. He could scatter them and run them down at leisure, sinking more ships in a few hours, perhaps, than he had done in all his weary months at sea. And the American coast was near enough for the British seamen to make safety in their boats; the sea was calm and likely to be so for hours to come – his scruples were satisfied so far as the lives of the merchant seamen were concerned.

Conjecture. It is all conjecture. The motivating thoughts behind Langsdorff's conduct will never be known. The papers which might have revealed them were later burned by accident when a young officer misinterpreted an instruction from his captain.

No man is consistent in all his actions, and this day Langsdorff made a miscalculation that was to bring gladness to the hearts of his country's enemies – a miscalculation as great as that which had caused the long-range shelling of the *Doric Star*, permitting her to radio a warning of a raider attack.

Captain Langsdorff had been in his bridge cabin, resting or sleeping, when dawn came to fling light into the battle area. On deck was his Arado float plane, which had been his eyes on previous occasions when his radar had failed him. But this day it was out of action, dismantled on the deck where mechanics had been attempting repairs the previous evening. Events were conspiring against the German captain. If he had had his Arado, the secrets over the horizon would have been fully known to him.

Would he then have run for it?

One of his lookouts had swept his arc of the horizon,

hesitated, and then come back. A long pause while he stared and the light brightened. Then suddenly a call to the bridge, "Ship on the starboard bow!"

Langsdorff was called from his cabin. The officer of the watch had known of the expectations regarding the *Highland Monarch*, and perhaps assumed that his commander's plans for interception had been nicely estimated. Perhaps the ease with which they had plundered and got safely away made for a confidence this morning that amounted to carelessness.

Langsdorff stared through his binoculars. The ship was seventeen miles away, his rangefinders now reported. He gave the order, "Action stations!" and the rattler sounded throughout the ship, bringing her crew in a mad, jostling rush to their places in battle.

More masts. A yell from the lookout startled them with the inference behind his echoing words. More than one ship was over the horizon. The convoy?

Still the *Graf Spee* slipped through the Atlantic waters at a comfortable cruising speed, holding on her course towards the unknown ships. Then came identification – and shock. An officer was checking the tall masts and super-structure just lifting above the horizon now, and the reference book said this was no destroyer, but a cruiser, and only the British *Exeter* had such tall masts as that. The *Exeter*, with six 8-inch guns.

Before Langsdorff had time to assimilate this news, a further shout of identification came down from the lookout. The other slender masts *were* those of two destroyers, it was reported.

Langsdorff's orders were to run from foes such as these, one British cruiser and two destroyers, but – an argument against the later charge of cowardice – in defiance of all his instructions, he would not change course at that moment. They saw him staring ahead through his binoculars, deliberately steering into an action which he could have avoided. Finally he turned and called his officers to him.

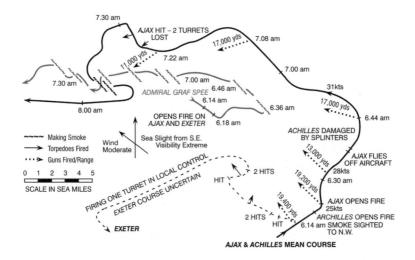

The Battle of the River Plate, 13 December 1939.

Such a concentration of warships could only indicate a convoy, he argued. All right, they would quickly take care of the *Exeter* and dispose of the destroyers if they got in the way. Here was the chance of a lifetime, a convoy inadequately protected, which they could sink at will. This day's events would be a major disaster in British maritime history. This day the *Graf Spee* would come into her own.

He kept his course. …

He, Captain Langsdorff. It was all in the British Admiralty's files about him, everything … except the knowledge that he would twice behave unpredictably and so bring battle upon himself.

Langsdorff was nearly forty-six, this thirteenth day of December, 1939. He had been born on March 20, 1894, a man destined for the sea.

His had been an honourable career, and because he was an intelligent and likeable man he had received promotion all through the years when it was denied others. A man had to be good to be given command of one of Hitler's finest ships, and all during his service he had impressed others with his talent and ability.

It was in April, 1912, that he had entered the Imperial Navy of Germany, at a time when another would-be dictator was preparing for war. During that war which smashed forever the German hope of mastery at sea, Langsdorff first served as a Sub-Lieutenant, then Adjutant and Torpedo Officer in the *Medusa*; then Adjutant and Signals Officer in the *Grosser Kurfürst*.

Later he became Commandant in Auxiliary Minesweeping Flotilla, North Sea, and then Commandant of Mine-sweepers M.36 and then M.76 until the end of the war. On December 25, 1917, he was promoted Lieutenant his last promotion in a navy that was not again to be called "Imperial". Soon it was to become the target of, first, men who feared it, and then of men who wanted it because it could help to bring the power for which political maniacs crave.

Langsdorff's career was not helped by the limitations of Germany's naval strength after the Versailles Treaty, yet promotion came steadily his way. On April 1, 1922, he was promoted Lieutenant-Commander; in 1925 he acted as Liaison Officer between the Navy and Army; and in 1932 he became Adjutant to the Minister of Defence, a rank corresponding to that of Naval Secretary to the First Lord of the British Admiralty. To be so singled out for promotion, Langsdorff had to have talent.

Langsdorff was not in command of the *Graf Spee* when she stole the headlines at the Spithead Review of 1937, though apparently he attended the ceremony in some capacity. He joined the ship in 1938 as Staff Officer to the Commander-in-Chief of the German Fleet, Admiral Carls. Later that year he took command of the pocket battleship.

On August 21, 1939, he said goodbye to his wife and brought his ship out of Wilhelmshaven, knowing there was to be war and he was starting on a voyage which would be long and hazardous and from which there was possibly no return.

Captain Langsdorff had the highest opinion of the British Navy which had smashed the Imperial German fleet in which he had first served.

Quite apparently he knew, when he left Germany, that the international situation was such that there was likely to be a war involving Britain, and he knew, then, full well what hazards were involved by his rôle as raider.

So far he had been lucky, all successes and not a scratch to his paintwork. In Berlin they were delighted with his cruise, and were hinting at his successes in the Press, though for the moment they were not able to mention Langsdorff or the *Graf Spee* in the news. Lucky Langsdorff.

Lucky until the thirteenth of December, 1939.

But even at 0600 on the thirteenth, Langsdorff did not know that his run of luck had ended. While the *Graf Spee* vibrated to the acceleration of her powerful engines, he conferred with his officers and detailed his plan of action. The *Exeter* first. She was going to be hounded out of the battle before she had time to know what had hit her. Then the destroyers. ...

His battle ensigns were being run up, proud streaming swastikas that never did any man any good. While simultaneously his lookouts reported the battle ensign of the *Exeter* fluttering from her mast-head ... a cleaner flag, a flag still able to command more respect and loyalty than any other on earth.

Exeter had thrown up her challenge – no problems of running away here. The *Graf Spee* had been seen, and the fight was on. From the moment the *Exeter* saw her – *Exeter* with her greater turn of speed – the *Graf Spee* could no longer avoid battle.

It was at this moment when he knew it was too late to alter his decision, too late to slide away before being detected, that a series of reports from his look-outs must have turned the brightness of his morning's optimism into a mood of awful, pulsating doubt.

The first report that reached him said the sea was clear behind the oncoming warships. *There was no convoy, and his risk was being taken for nothing.*

Then other, swift, seemingly merciless reports. The warships were diverging, an ominous sign, racing in now to get the German battleship between them.

But finally came *the* report that must have filled him with dismay, though he never showed it to his officers. Those other masts were not destroyers'. They were cruisers'!

At that news, Langsdorff must have regretted the impetuous decision to attack. Three British cruisers – little fellows compared with his own mighty ship ... but British. He knew then he would not get out of this battle with a few minor injuries, because that sort of luck just did not happen against the well-disciplined, finely-trained British Navy.

Yet Langsdorff gave no order to turn away from battle. He sought battle, perhaps hoping to crush his opponents before they could do him any injury, and now his ship was racing in at speed for the kill.

Abruptly, Langsdorff gave an order that would start the Battle of the River Plate. His 11-inch guns swung to aim at *Exeter*. Suddenly, the ship shuddered and men's ears seemed to crack as a weight of sound smote them, then the first mighty shells went hurtling from the gun barrels, high into the air, on an arc calculated to take them exactly as far as *Exeter*.

On the morning of December 13, the unfortunate – yet not too unfortunate – prisoners aboard the *Graf Spee* awoke to the sound of the alarm rattler and the running of feet overhead. It was a depressing noise, and most had heard it several times before.

"Another poor devil caught," they must have thought, stirring from their blankets and sitting up. That was their immediate reaction to the familiar sounds of men taking action stations: the *Graf Spee* had trapped another merchantman. Soon they would be having to find space for more prisoners, and that was a problem as much to them as to the good-natured Langsdorff. They were uncomfortably crowded, here in the compartment below the for'ard turret, even without the addition of fellow victims. Still, it would be nice to see a few new faces and hear the latest news. ...

All at once the prisoners began to scramble hurriedly to their feet, instinctively feeling that this time there was something different in the way the *Graf Spee*'s crew had gone into action. This time there seemed an urgency about the way men ran and shouted to each other that was in contrast with other occasions when Action Stations had been sounded. In that moment the prisoners began to get suspicions, and while these brought eager, leaping hope into their hearts, they carried with them dread.

Suddenly a German officer ran in and shouted, "Gentlemen, I am afraid I must leave you to your own devices today." With these startling words, he turned and ran out again, the doors were slammed behind him and the prisoners knew they were being locked in.

For an instant they looked at each other while their brains swiftly assimilated all the implications behind the officer's words and actions. Their first quick suspicion was right, they realised – the *Graf Spee* had run into trouble and was about to be involved in a fight. Someone started to cheer. The Navy was out there, gunning for the German who had sunk their ships. Then the cheer stopped. They looked round their compartment. They were behind armour, they knew, and Langsdorff had assured them they were in the safest part of the ship. But what if the ship was severely damaged and went down, and they were locked in a steel strong-box. ... ?

The men stopped thinking about it. The Navy was out there, and by God, they were supporting them, there in the heart of the enemy ship.

All at once, completely unheralded, a wave of sound hit the metal walls of their prison and seemed to send them all staggering. The immediate thought of many of them was that the *Graf Spee* had either been already hit in the fight or had suffered a severe explosion. Seconds later their bemused wits seized hold of the truth. The explosion that had come with such startling suddenness had been the firing of one of the mighty 11-inch guns above their heads. They were right under the turret, and for the next eighty minutes they were going to suffer from the thunderous roar and concussion of those enormous guns.

Aboard *Exeter*, when the rattler sounded for action stations, many of the men thought it to be the usual practice or false alarm. Consequently, it was with picturesque and lurid comment that they witnessed an explosion in the sea just short of the ship. This then was *it*, the real thing. Any lingering sleep went from them with the realisation that now they were fighting for their lives.

A signal was seen fluttering from the *Ajax*. This battle, too, had started with a historical injunction – "England," signalled Commodore Harwood, "expects that every man will do his duty". Nelson's signal at the Battle of Trafalgar, October 21, 1805.

The ships were on diverging courses now, the Ist Division (*Ajax* and *Achilles*) skimming like startled seal birds, closing range rapidly, working up to top speed, though it would take them almost an hour to attain it; the *Exeter* hauling out of line and altering course to west-ward in accordance with Harwood's pre-arranged plan. The British cruisers were intent on getting on either side of the German – nutcrackers to smash a nut, but a mighty tough nut to crack, they knew.

Three sleek light cruisers of the Royal Navy went streaking through the placid near-tropical sea towards the mighty pocket battleship. The big guns of the *Graf Spee* were on *Exeter*. The first ponderous flight of 670-pound 11-inch shells had fallen short. The next salvo was already on its way as the gun crews aboard *Exeter* prepared to fire their smaller but still powerful guns. The range had been 19,400 yards when the pocket battleship first fired and it was lessening rapidly as all four ships raced towards each other.

Less than nineteen thousand yards range. ...

It was incredible. Langsdorff was throwing away his advantages, was virtually nullifying the thought that had gone into the design and construction of his pocket battleship. Afterwards Commodore Harwood said that Langsdorff gave them their chance to survive because he came in when he should have stood away ... the British cruisers' prospects were as small as that.

The *Graf Spee* should have fought a long-distance battle, but didn't. Langsdorff should have kept out of damaging range of the smaller British guns for as long as possible, instead of playing into the hands of the British and closing to a range where even 8-inch guns could hurt.

For a quarter-of-an-hour after sighting the *Exeter*'s mast tops, Langsdorff went head on into battle. If he had turned and run for it – a tactical manœuvre – forcing the British cruisers to catch up on him slowly, all the time within range of his damaging guns and yet mostly beyond effective distance of the British, he could probably have pounded the light cruisers for the better part of an hour with little risk of damage to himself. In that hour his own accurate gunnery must surely have disposed of his enemies, or at least have crippled most of them.

But Langsdorff, unpredictable in his tactics in the last days of his life, chose to bring his vessel immediately within range of all three British ships.

True, success was all with him at first. His second salvo fell directly astern. The third and fourth salvoes also missed thunderously, and by this time *Exeter* had opened fire – the time, 0621, seven minutes after sighting the battleship's distant smoke, and only four minutes after the *Graf Spee*'s first 11-inch salvo.

Racing to intercept the *Graf Spee*, the 1st Division saw their sister ship plunge through shell bursts that threw up the sea around her. The British ship was twisting and turning, taking evasive action to throw off the enemy gunners, but all the time moving relentlessly in on the more powerful battleship, her guns belching smoke as she hurled her 8-inch shells at the *Graf Spee*. *Exeter* had closed to about 17,500 yards by now, but her first salvoes were short.

To *Ajax* and *Achilles*, there could be one end to that battle, even though the *Graf Spee* was needlessly coming to close quarters with the *Exeter*. All the German need do was to keep his main armament concentrated on the West Country cruiser, and within minutes the *Exeter* would surely be blown clean out of the water. British gunners would have done it, they felt certain.

But almost as soon as Langsdorff had opened his broadsides on the *Exeter* – 4,200 pounds of spinning steel and high explosive in each six 11-inch gun salvo – he ordered one turret to open fire on the *Ajax*.

Here was another mistaken decision on the part of Captain Langsdorff. Swinging from one target to another took time, and time was friendly to the British because it enabled the smaller cruisers to close in to a range when they could use their 6-inch guns. Langsdorff, the strategists were to argue later, should have made up his mind on his tactics before opening fire, and not have started changing targets so soon after the battle had begun.

Langsdorff, the same experts were agreed, should have concentrated all his main armament on the *Exeter* until she was disposed of. As it was, changing from one target to another (Langsdorff was to do this repeatedly over the first few minutes) again threw away further advantages inherent in the design of the pocket battleship.

Ajax was under fire from the *Graf Spee* from 0618, and then *Achilles* became a target. The battleship's secondary armament now concentrated upon the smaller cruisers – they were the *Graf Spee*'s 5.9-inch guns, only fractionally less powerful than *Ajax* and *Achilles'* main armament of 6-inch guns.

Langsdorff paved the way to his own destruction by his indecision in those critical first minutes; for it gave *Exeter*, closing in at high speed, chance to shorten the range still further – gave her gun crews time to load and fire, load and fire yet again, and do more harm to the enemy than they realised. Not that *Exeter* was out of the battle; some 11-inch guns still ranged her, and the quarter-ton shells thundered all too close to the British cruiser in spite of her captain's brilliant evasive tactics. And in time they *would* hit, and then there would be death and destruction aboard and everyone knew it.

For the moment, though, the *Exeter* was unscathed, and Captain Bell and all his crew knew one thought only in those vital minutes as the two warships came head-on towards each other – "Get the German before he gets us!" Punish the *Graf Spee* before her commander brought all his guns to bear on his most dangerous opponent. Try for the lucky shot which might miraculously find a weak spot in the battleship's supposed invulnerability.

Exeter came in hell-for-leather towards her bigger opponent. She, the biggest cruiser, was the most dangerous, and she wanted to draw the enemy fire upon herself and give the smaller vessels chance to work in to closer range. She drew the enemy fire, and all at once began the appalling, murderous thrashing of the gallant *Exeter*, a thrashing that was almost to destroy her as a fighting unit within minutes of the beginning of the battle.

The thrashing started for the *Exeter* at 0622. An 11-inch shell exploded in the sea, close amidships. Above the noise of their own 8-inch guns firing, they heard the explosion and then saw men go down in death and agony as 11-inch shell-casing tore great holes through their own comparatively thin armour-plate.

In a second the *Exeter* was a shambles. Fires started, electrical circuits were put out of action. Communications were damaged and their aircraft and searchlights riddled and rendered useless; the aircraft, in fact, had to be jettisoned overboard because of the danger from their burst petrol tanks.

And men had been killed. The starboard torpedo tube's crew died all together, and in other parts of the ship the flying steel sawed through limbs and bodies and left a trail of dead and dying.

It was *Exeter's* first taste of the power of those mighty 11-inch guns, and lucky they were to have been hit with a near miss and not a direct hit. The *Exeter* seemed to shudder at the impact, and then went leaping closer towards the violently zig-zagging *Graf Spee*, her guns firing salvo after salvo, almost twice as fast as the return fire of those dreaded 11-inch German weapons: it was this fierce and accurate fire from *Exeter* which made the raider take such violently evasive action, and because of it her marksmanship suffered. Because she suffered, back came her main armament to concentrate on the 8-inch gun cruiser, thus permitting the smaller ships to get closer still.

All the while that the *Exeter* was taking the main fire, the smaller cruisers were working up to top speed and closing in to a range when their own comparatively puny 6-inch guns would be able to hurt.

More shells hurtled around *Exeter,* and then again an 11-inch projectile smashed into her – this time a direct hit. But again she was lucky; this time incredibly lucky. A mighty 670-pound shell suddenly smashed through the deck abaft B turret, sped through the Sick Bay now filling with wounded, and smashed its way out through the ship's side without bursting. A few men were injured by the splinters following the shell's swift passage through the ship, but everyone knew that luck had been on their side. If it had burst, the death roll would have been high, and the effect on the ship disastrous.

But the next 11-inch shell did burst on the ship. The time was 0625. To the crew, going through their gun drill like robots, the action already seemed to have been in progress for hours, but in fact only eleven minutes had passed since their first sight of the *Graf Spee*'s smoke that early dawn. The *Exeter* had just fired her eighth salvo – nearly three tons of high explosive had been hurled at the frantically dodging German battleship in a matter of five minutes. Then the British cruiser sustained a direct hit and with one round was virtually knocked out of the battle.

Two minutes before, the *Graf Spee* had altered course, turning violently to port so that she could fight a starboard action. Now the German was no longer running head on into battle but was trying to parallel the course of the 1st Division. It was tactics that Langsdorff should have employed from the beginning, and it looked ominous for the British ships.

Chapter 13

H.M.S. Exeter is Pounded

The violence of that exploding 11-inch shell was terrible to see. It burst against B gun turret, knocking out both guns and killing eight of the crew; the armour plate was ripped off as if it had been wet cardboard, and the miracle was that anyone remained alive after the violence of the projectile bursting against the turret.

But that one shell did even greater damage elsewhere. The flying shell-splinters riddled the bridge and killed all personnel on it except the captain and two officers. It also wrecked the wheelhouse communications, and this now meant that the *Exeter* was a ship out of control, madly racing on towards its still unharmed adversary.

There was no thought of giving up the fight, though. *Exeter* had some guns left to fire and all her speed to keep up with the enemy. Confusion turned into something like order as Captain Bell, wounded in the face, raced to the after conning position and controlled the ship through a relay of men ending in the lower steering position.

By word of mouth, passed on through a link of ten men, Captain Bell took his ship back into battle.

The *Exeter* swung back on course and opened up with her remaining guns. The *Graf Spee* saw that she had severely hurt her biggest opponent and tried her damnedest to polish her off. Her guns ranged the gallant *Exeter*, trying to land another shell which might completely put her out of the fight, but for a few more minutes the West Country ship survived, and in that time, *Ajax*, still only travelling at 27 knots, managed to close to about 15,000 yards. At that range even her 6-inch shells, mere 100-pounders, would not be insignificant.

The *Exeter*, on fire and to Langsdorff clearly very badly hit, was lessening the distance between her and the German cruiser, and because of it Langsdorff continued to fire his main armament at her. Now, though, in spite of the appalling damage she had suffered, the *Exeter* gunners were beginning to land on the battleship. Each time a round exploded on the *Graf Spee*, the commander on the aft control tower shouted out the news to his men. The guns' crews, fighting "blind" in their turrets, cheered each triumphant cry and worked like fury to maintain their rate of fire.

Then *Exeter* landed the hit of the battle, the blow that did more damage than any other shell landing on the enemy. The *Graf Spee*, weaving violently though she was to dodge the British shells, was being bombarded pretty intensively now by the guns of all three British cruisers. However, apart from making a seemingly nervous German crew more jittery, the shells were not doing much damage on the thickly-armoured *Graf Spee*.

Then one lucky 8-inch *Exeter* shell exploded right on the *Graf Spee*'s Control Tower, a smack between the eyes for the enemy and for some time altering the odds much more in favour of the smaller vessels.

The shell which exploded on the *Graf Spee*'s Control Tower killed many officers and highly skilled instrument operators, as well as wrecking the important range finder and other instruments and damaging communications. Until temporary repairs could be effected, for the next crucial part of the engagement, the *Graf Spee*'s main armament had to fire independently and with consequently less accuracy. Again it gave respite to the heroic crew of the *Exeter*, still ploughing forward, still intent on taking the fight to the enemy.

The morning's brightness became clouded with the smoke of battle; the serenity of dawn in the placid South Atlantic was ripped asunder with the constant roar of mighty guns hurling death at each other. Now the British ships were seeming to leap closer to their opponent, like eager hounds wanting to sink their teeth into their enemy's throat. And the *Graf Spee* seemed somehow befuddled by the ferocity of the attack, the unrelenting approach of the smaller enemy in the face of her terrible 11-inch armament. Later the British crews were to learn of the demoralisation of the young and inexperienced German sailors at the battering they were being subjected to. Around them, comrades were falling in agony, wounded and dying – or dead. Yet had they not been assured that no ship could ever hurt them? Hadn't Langsdorff said they would never fight a sea battle, because there was nothing at sea that could take them on effectively?

Bewildered, they knew they were being hurt. Nowhere near as much as the *Exeter*, if they had known it – *Exeter's* injuries were to exceed those of the other three ships engaged – but even if they had known it, the Germans would have found little consolation in the thought.

In desperation, it seemed, Langsdorff now also put some of his secondary armament on the largest British cruiser, as if he wanted to silence those 8-inch guns at all costs, even at the price of easing up on the *Ajax* and *Achilles*. Yet, cunningly dodging the furious storm of German shells, the *Exeter* still came racing after the *Graf Spee*, and her own accurate gunnery showed in burst after burst against the heavy armour of the battleship.

It seemed a long time to the battling crews – a long time because near-misses were riddling the *Exeter's* sides and causing havoc among the gallant crew. Yet only seven minutes had passed from the time that *Exeter* had fired her first broadside, when she received her second and third direct hits.

Both were 11-inch shells. Both created tremendous havoc.

The miracle was that *Exeter*'s engines remained unharmed so that in spite of the explosions she could still keep up with the fight.

The first mighty shell exploded on the sheet anchor, tearing an enormous hole in the side of the ship just above the water line and starting a fire in the paint room. Flames spread instantly, in spite of the efforts of the handicapped crew to fight them; smoke rolled out over the ship, announcing to the enemy her distress. Through the smoke and flames could be seen the twisted, mangled forms of more dead, huddled and broken where the force of the explosion had hurled them. Amid the torn plating, the broken pipes and trailing wires the scene was nightmarish.

The other 11-inch shell landed almost immediately after the first one. It smashed through the *Exeter*'s deck and exploded, doing incredible damage. The ship seemed to stagger in her stride, then once again plunged on. Her captain knew no other thought than that he should attack the enemy, and that day it was the spirit and determination of men who lived by tradition, more than guns and armour-plating, which was winning the battle.

Captain Bell, even in the distress of his battered ship, saw a moment when torpedoes might be effective. They were fired, sleek missiles of death that travelled undeviatingly towards their target. For two minutes they kept on their course, and now it looked as though they were going to hit the pocket battleship. Then, almost at the last moment, the *Graf Spee* changed course with a violence which said the torpedoes had been spotted, and the missiles went wide.

The firing of those torpedoes had a decisive effect upon the battle. As if shocked by the nearness of his escape; as if reminded that even a battleship could be severely damaged by one lucky torpedo hit, Langsdorff broke off the battle. No doubt about it, at 0634, seventeen minutes only since he had gone boldly into battle, his great guns flashing awesomely at the smaller warships, Langsdorff decided to quit. It might have been temporary; it might have been good strategy considering the state of his Control Tower. It could not have been cowardice, and it must have been consideration for his ship and her crew.

Whatever the reason, immediately following the scare from the firing of the *Exeter*'s torpedoes, the *Graf Spee* was seen to lay a smoke screen and hide herself within it. The *Ajax* and *Achilles*, also taking advantage of the smoke screen to come to closer range, were first to realise that the *Graf Spee* had made another violent change of course and now was speeding northwards, away from the fight.

The British cruisers promptly altered course, too. They weren't going to let the German raider, who had done so much damage to British shipping, get out of the fight.

Even so, running away though she might be – tactics which would have been correct and more profitable to her if she had chosen to employ them when the British cruisers weren't within range – the *Graf Spee*'s main and secondary armaments still kept up a heavy fire, and very quickly further success came to the German.

Exeter was still the principal target, and at 0640 tragedy ranged again aboard her. Two more direct hits were received from the German's big guns – two 11-inch shells exploded with stunning violence, this time quite positively putting the cruiser out of action. She had done her part well, hurting the battleship more than she knew at the time, and bringing the raider's fire upon herself to save the smaller cruisers. She had fought for twenty minutes and was now a wreck of a ship, but the honours of battle were hers at that moment.

The first of the two direct hits smashed open A turret, hitting the right gun. The second burst in the Chief Petty Officers' flat and did a great amount of damage including the starting of a fire. All compass repeaters were now out of action, and Captain Bell was using a boat's compass. With dauntless courage, crippled though they were, he still maintained pursuit of the *Graf Spee*, though he could only operate Y turret, firing in local control. As an effective fighting force *Exeter* was finished, but while she could still distract some of the enemy fire from the lighter cruisers Captain Bell would not withdraw from the battle.

Again he fired his port torpedoes, missed, but saw the violently evasive action of the German ship, and then a second smoke screen go up. The *Exeter* did have a nuisance value, it seemed.

Achilles and *Ajax* were not escaping unscathed, however. Like agile terriers snapping at the heels of a startled horse, they came boring in, zig-zagging and exerting their skill to spoil the aim of the enemy gunners. Lieutenant E.D.G. Lewin, pilot of one of the Seafox aircraft aboard the *Ajax*, with Lieutenant R. Kearney as observer, took off in his plane even though he had to be catapulted into the air without pause to the firing of their own guns – a remarkable and distinctly dangerous feat. He sped away to report on the ships' gunnery, but for technical reasons was unable to establish radio contact with the squadron until a quarter of an hour later, thus not being the assistance he had expected to be.

Suddenly a salvo of 11-inch shells burst in the sea near to *Achilles*, and just as in the case of the *Exeter*, massive shell splinters gouged their way through men and steel alike. Captain Parry was knocked down on the bridge, unconscious for a few moments and bleeding profusely from head and leg wounds. When he came to he discovered that the Gunnery Control was not functioning and the guns were silent. Inside the Director Control Turret many of the men had been killed, and all others stunned or wounded and for the moment incapable of action. After Control was immediately ordered to take over, and *Achilles* swung into battle once more. Some time later the Director Control Turret was got in order, and effective firing began again.

Exeter, still in the battle, was shipping water forward and was down by the bows three feet, with a list approaching ten degrees to starboard. Only Y turret and one 4-inch gun could be fired, but whenever possible their crews kept them in action. At 0648 she was again badly hit by two 11-inch projectiles, not to mention other shells from the *Graf Spee*'s secondary armament. Now she was dropping astern, because at speed she was shipping too much water, but for almost another hour she kept her one Y turret firing at the enemy until flooding caused a failure of power to the turret. Only then was Y turret silent.

For almost an hour the *Exeter* had borne the brunt of the battle, drawing the fire upon herself and inflicting severe damage upon a supposedly invincible ship. At the end of that time more men were dead aboard *Exeter* than in all the other ships, including the *Graf Spee*, engaged in the battle. Nearly forty were already dead, and eventually over sixty would die as a result of *Exeter*'s daring and gallantry.

The Germans had the invincible ship, but the British the invincible men.

Even now Captain Bell would not withdraw from the battle. Settling in the water, hardly a gun capable of firing, losing ground in the chase, he tried to keep up with the fight, his battle ensign still flying.

Chapter 14

Exeter Is Ordered Out of Battle

Langsdorff was now clearly running away. This was puzzling to his opponents who were not to know how accurate had been their gunnery, and how much damage their smaller shells had done to the battleship. Aboard the *Graf Spee* a bewildered crew weren't sure of their captain's tactics either, their morale shattered by the swiftness of the events of the past hour. Never had they expected to run away in such fashion, and yet they were on the run. Behind them came two small cruisers, taking up the fight now the *Exeter* was receding from the battle. They were coming into suicidal range, and the gunnery of those 6-inch British guns was demoralisingly accurate.

Time after time the battleship ranged with her full armament concentrating now upon two ships instead of three, yet by superb seamanship the cruisers mostly escaped injury. Now the violently zig-zagging German raider frequently employed smoke screens to protect her from the more rapidly firing British guns, but with great daring both *Achilles* and *Ajax* turned them to their own advantage by coming to closer quarters under cover of them. Eight times in one hour, in fact, the fleeing *Graf Spee* threw up smoke screens.

At 0646, however, there had been a significant change of course on the part of the *Graf Spee*. Her flight north became suddenly a mad rush westward, towards the coast of South America.

The tactics became puzzling as minutes passed and the German raider maintained her course. In the British ships it was not understandable why the German should head for the coast – safety for a raider lay in the open sea, not near to land.

In time it began to appear as if Langsdorff's intention was to make for a South American port, and then the mystification deepened. If he took the *Graf Spee* into port he ran the risk of being bottled up. Why, then, was he doing it?

Why didn't he turn even now and polish off the *Exeter*, then make a running fight of it all day while heading deeper into the Atlantic, hoping that in the darkness of night he could give his pursuers the slip? Those were the tactics he should have employed, at least that was the opinion of his pursuers. But to run for the temporary safety of a neutral port – that was beyond comprehension.

Afterwards, in attempting to understand Langsdorff's decision to run for port, it was stated that his fuel position was precarious. This theory propounded an urgent need for refuelling, yet it is unbelievable that the *Graf Spee* was within a few hours of the end of her reserves. She had taken on oil on December 6, and should have had several more days' fuel left. In any event, she ran all day, proving that she had enough fuel to take her into the hours of darkness, and the *Altmark* could not have been too far away.

But Langsdorff, for his own reasons – which might have been that he was sick of battle and slaughter – deliberately took his vessel into a bottle-neck tighter than that provided by two small cruisers out at sea.

By 0712 the two British cruisers had worked up to their utmost speed, and now Commodore Harwood made a bold attempt to come in to quarters close enough for his 6-inch guns to cause serious damage. It might have been playing into his enemy's hands, for with the *Exeter* withdrawing from the fight, all the *Graf Spee*'s 11-inch guns could now be concentrated upon the remaining pursuers.

Every gun that could be brought to bear upon the *Graf Spee* was firing as *Ajax* and *Achilles* closed in on the German raider. The noise was tremendous and the ships shuddered to the violence of their broadsides. Three times a minute their 6-inch guns hurled their load of death at the enemy, with smaller guns contributing to the battle sounds as they came within effective range.

At 0716 it was observed that the *Graf Spee* had made a drastic alteration to her course under cover of smoke. Suddenly she was seen to break from it travelling at top speed, almost due south, and heading directly towards the crippled, helpless *Exeter.*

It seemed to Commodore Harwood that Langsdorff had changed his mind about running away and was racing in to finish off the big cruiser. At once he ordered *Ajax* and *Achilles* to close in so as to take the fire from *Exeter.*

Perhaps it had been in Langsdorff's mind to polish off one of his annoying pursuers; perhaps he was going all out to sink the *Exeter.* But almost from the moment he came out of the smoke screen he was under furious fire from the two cruisers. True, his own 11-inch guns straddled the *Ajax* three times at the comparatively close range of only 11,000 yards, but the fire from his secondary armament was ragged and appeared consistently to be going over, between the two cruisers.

The 6-inch shells from *Ajax* and *Achilles* found their target. Up above in the Seafox aircraft Kearney kept signalling, "Good shot," as hit after hit registered. Soon a red glow was seen amidships in the German raider where a fierce fire was burning.

Perhaps the sustained and accurate fire of the cruisers daunted Langsdorff and turned him from his target; at any rate, abruptly he made another violent change of course and, zig-zagging constantly, resumed his westward flight towards the South American coast.

At 0725, however, the balance was swung dramatically in favour of the German. Suddenly *Ajax* seemed to stop in the water as a mighty explosion rocked her. An 11-inch shell had scored a direct hit on the after superstructure. The shell smashed its way through various cabins, then X turret trunk, wrecking the turret machinery below the gunhouse, before finally bursting in Commodore Harwood's sleeping cabin. Some part of the bursting shell also struck Y barbette and jammed the turret.

Thus one hit put both X and Y turrets of *Ajax* out of action, killing four and wounding six of X turret's crew. Now the *Graf Spee* was opposed by virtually only one and a half cruisers, and the odds of battle were well in her favour.

Commodore Harwood, unscathed amid the debris aboard his flagship, thought now that Langsdorff was in fact turning to attack the cruisers, and promptly ordered a broadside of torpedoes to dissuade such attentions. At 0727 *Ajax*, still able to maintain her speed, turned to starboard and fired four torpedoes. The range was only 9,000 yards now, uncomfortably close to the *Graf Spee*'s big guns, though a long range for the torpedoes, of course.

They missed. *Graf Spee* must have seen them coming, for suddenly she turned violently 130 degrees to port, and did not resume her westward course for a few minutes. All the same, the German raider seemed to lose her recent confidence and did not continue the threatened attack. The Royal Navy was still dictating the battle, inferior in armament though they were. The *Graf Spee* was bolting behind the protection of yet another smoke screen.

At 0731, from the Seafox aircraft, Lieutenant Kearney signalled, "Torpedoes approaching". He then added, "They will pass ahead of you". The *Graf Spee* was trying to get her own back on the *Ajax* now.

All the same, in spite of Kearney's assurances, *Ajax* took evasive action appropriate to the danger concerned and the torpedoes ran far off their mark.

The cruisers were harrying the *Graf Spee* from their closest range of the battle now. Boldly they had raced in to 8,000 yards and were pounding the big battleship with everything they had. Time after time they saw their shells burst against the *Graf Spee*.

But 6-inch shells, it was now all too apparent, could not penetrate the thick armour protecting the bigger ship. They were a damned nuisance to the German, but weren't going to cripple her.

All the raider's guns were still in action, and again she was firing with her full armament at the cruisers so close to her – her full armament ... those six 11-inch guns, those eight 5.9-inch guns, almost as big as *Ajax* and *Achilles'* biggest, and six 4-inch anti-aircraft guns.

Brilliant seamanship was saving the cruisers, but it could not go on indefinitely. They could not appear to hurt the *Graf Spee* and inevitably she would score further direct hits and blow them out of the water. Commodore Harwood had to make a decision.

A report from *Ajax* appeared to dictate further strategy – she appeared to be running out of ammunition. The report indicated that *Ajax* had only twenty per cent of her ammunition left; later it was realised that the report referred only to A turret which had been firing almost constantly throughout the action and the other three turrets had more ammunition left.

So Commodore Harwood ordered, "Break off the action", and the two cruisers immediately began to go out of range. They were still firing as they withdrew, and the *Graf Spee* was employing all her effective armament against the cruisers.

They were breaking off the engagement when suddenly one of the raider's last salvoes hit *Ajax*. The 11-inch salvo straddled her, and with a crash one of the shells hit the main topmast and brought it down. All the aerials were torn away, and for some time the *Ajax* could not transmit radio signals until jury aerials were rigged.

Making smoke, the two cruisers now pulled rapidly out of range, and then, at a distance of about 30,000 yards from the German battleship, they proceeded to shadow her all during the day of December 13, *Achilles* on her starboard quarter, *Ajax* to port of her.

Exeter slowly began to repair as much of the damage as possible. At 1105 she signalled a report to Commodore Harwood – "All turrets out of action. Flooded forward up to No.14 bulkhead, but can still do eighteen knots."

Harwood signalled back, "Proceed to the Falkland Islands at whatever speed is possible without straining your bulkheads". He wasn't going to let the *Exeter* remain in the fight. So, a wreck of a once fine warship, the *Exeter* went out of the Battle of the River Plate, ministering to her wounded, and wrapping her many dead ready for burial.

Lieutenant Lewin came down from the skies at 0912, his role as spotter over with the cessation of firing. Now it was a chase, a long-range shadowing, and not for several more hours was there any further fighting. Conditions weren't easy for picking up the Seafox plane, but brilliant manœuvring on the part of pilot and ship's captain effected the operation swiftly and safely and without loss of time.

In Berlin, Raeder and Hitler were receiving reports of the engagement and of Langsdorff's decision to run for port. It must have been a stupefying blow to the German leaders, to learn that their mighty warship was running from British Navy cruisers, and doubtless from that minute began attempts to find a face-saving formula: a country just precipitated into war could not be expected to be told of this dramatic reverse to their fortunes so early in the proceedings.

Commodore Harwood now sent a signal of recall to the *Cumberland* in the Falkland Islands ... a thousand miles away, and yet the only other British ship capable of reaching them in time to assist in the battle ahead. As it was, the passage was to take her over thirty hours, proceeding at full speed, to reach the area. That meant, so far as *Achilles* and the battered *Ajax* were concerned, that if the bigger battleship showed fight, they would have to take her on unaided.

The *Graf Spee* did not for several hours show much fight.

True, at 1005 *Achilles* over-estimated the enemy's speed and found herself in at about 23,000 yards range, whereat the *Graf Spee*'s big guns suddenly erupted in wrath, firing two salvoes, the second of which fell uncomfortably close to the New Zealand-manned ship. Hastily *Achilles* made smoke and sped to a more comfortable range. Getting hit at this stage in the proceedings would not have been in the interests of anyone except Captain Langsdorff and a crew who needed something to improve their morale.

It was shortly after this time that *Exeter* was ordered away to the Falkland Islands, which *Cumberland* was just quitting at great speed. It took her three days to get there, a battered ship almost helpless to defend herself. When she came off Port Stanley they failed to recognise her because of her changed appearance, and guns defending the harbour were manned, ready to open fire on the suspicious warship.

But when they came into the berth quitted so recently by *Cumberland*, the gallant if weary crew received the welcome of their lives. Even seventeen years later men were to remember it, and say, "If nothing else, the people of the Falklands should get credit for the way they looked after us".

They were down at the harbour to receive the crew, with blankets and spare clothing, and hearts overflowing for men who had gone through so much and were still obviously suffering from the action. They took them into their homes and looked after the wounded, and there was nothing the good people of the Falklands could do was too much for the *Exeter* men.

Chapter 15

The S.S. Shakespeare

It was the prisoners aboard the *Graf Spee* who had the most anxious and uncomfortable time of any concerned in the battle. It was one thing to be on deck, fighting, but quite another to be trapped in a steel box beneath a thundering gun turret. Bemused and deafened, the time passed very slowly.

Sometimes the battleship heeled so violently that the alarmed prisoners were certain she had been hit and was sinking, on other occasions shells burst near to their prison and they felt the blast wave flood in on them.

Suddenly an exploding shell filled the room with debris as part of the bulkhead beam collapsed and the deck seemed to open. Then part of a skylight cover was blown away and they were able to obtain a view of a 6-inch gun wrecked outside.

As much as possible the prisoners maintained a watch through the opening. From the beginning they had the impression that the heart of the crew was not in this battle at all. To the prisoners, the Germans seemed miserable and fearful. They were very young, from what they could see, mere boys mostly of seventeen to twenty-two or three.

As the battle wore on, the watching prisoners saw wounded being dragged past their prison, and then the Germans began to pile their dead outside. It was a gruesome sight. After a time, in the heat of the day, the corpses began to decompose and the smell was bad even though the dead were washed down with a hose and disinfectant liberally strewn over them.

The effect of the dead and wounded appeared to be greater upon the crew of the *Graf Spee* than upon the British seamen, however. All over the place men were being sick, and a constant procession was being dragged into the lavatories, as if the sight of the slaughter was too much for the young Germans. Morale was low, and perhaps it was this that contributed to Langsdorff's decision to make for port. His crew weren't in fighting condition, though it might be asked why they weren't.

The prisoners had little opinion of the discipline aboard the German raider, and felt that it contributed to the lack of morale in time of battle.

They remembered what they had seen before the action, and it wasn't the kind of discipline they would have expected in the British Navy. Men used to smoke on the guns, and the lookouts often could be seen with cigarettes in their mouths. They noticed, too, that none of the junior officers saluted their seniors, and there was overmuch familiarity on the part of the men with their officers: friendliness makes for a happy ship, but not an atmosphere too free and easy, the prisoners often commented to themselves.

Curiously, Langsdorff did not appear to be very much in command of his ship, relying upon his second-in-command – a much more Prussian-type of officer, and yet discipline wasn't good. When the German crew went into battle, it seemed as though their morale wilted, and the prisoners, many of them ex-R.N. types, noted it grimly and thought they knew why.

No one came near the prisoners until four or five hours after the firing had stopped. This was when the battle had become a pursuit, with the *Graf Spee* fleeing steadily westward, and the two British cruisers shadowing from a distance.

Suddenly they heard someone outside shouting, "Are you

all right in there?" The presence of the prisoners had been remembered. They called back that they had not suffered any injury but were thirsty and hungry, not having eaten that day.

Half an hour later the door was unlocked and a German sailor brought in a dixie full of lime water and some black bread. That was all they got. Then the door was locked on them again. Later in the afternoon, the door was again unlocked and more lime juice, bread and two tins of sausage meat were brought in. It was explained to them that the galleys were out of action, and there was no hot food for anyone aboard the *Graf Spee*. Dismally, depressingly, the hours passed. When the firing was resumed, they stuck it out until evening. Then they slung their hammocks and crawled into them. They felt very helpless, lying there, listening to the thunder of guns overhead. They wondered how it was going to end, and weren't very happy about their prospects.

Shortly after the *Exeter* had been ordered out of the battle, Commodore Harwood received a signal from his opponent, Langsdorff. This was dramatic in itself, but it contained news which surprised the British commodore. The signal revealed that the pocket battleship they were pursuing was not the *Admiral Scheer*, as they thought, but, the *Graf Spee*.

The message read, "Please pick up lifeboats of English steamer". Only, when they came up there were no lifeboats to pick up.

Langsdorff had sighted an unfortunate British merchant-man right in her tracks, and promptly, even though in flight, set about sinking her. The ship was the S.S. *Shakespeare*, 5,000 tons, steaming towards the River Plate. The *Graf Spee* at once bore down upon her latest victim and fired a warning shot as an order for her to stop. Langsdorff then signalled to her captain to take to the boats with his crew, preparatory to his sinking the ship with a torpedo.

All this was watched from a great distance by the

Part of the superstructure of the German pocket battleship *Admiral Graf Spee*. The *Admiral Graf Spee* was the third and last *Panzerschiff* (armoured ship) of the Deutschland-class, whose ships were referred to as "pocket battleships" by the British. (Historic Military Press)

Above: The launching of the German pocket battleship *Admiral Graf Spee* at Wilhelmshaven, Germany, on 30 June 1934. (Historic Military Press)

Below: *Admiral Graf Spee* underway in the English Channel, August 1939. It was on the 21st of that month that *Graf Spee* departed Wilhelmshaven for the South Atlantic as a precautionary measure in case war broke out. In due course, on 26 September 1939, *Graf Spee* was ordered to leave her waiting area and commence hostilities against British merchant shipping. (US Naval Historical Center)

Above: Seen from the deck of Admiral *Graf Spee*, this dramatic picture, taken by a German cameraman, shows the final moments of the pocket battleship's first victim, the British steamer *Clement* seventy-five miles south-east of Pernambuco, Brazil. (Historic Military Press)

Above: The cruiser HMNZS *Achilles* seen from HMS *Ajax* at the Battle of the River Plate. Formerly part of the New Zealand Division of the Royal Navy, in October 1941 *Achilles* was transferred to the newly-formed Royal New Zealand Navy.

Above: *Admiral Graf Spee* anchored in Montevideo Harbour on 15 or 16 December 1939. The warship had entered the harbour shortly after midnight on 14 December. She soon became the centre of much attention, as the boats carrying sight-seers in this image testify. (US Naval Historical Center)

Below: *Admiral Graf Spee* in Montevideo Harbour after the Battle of River Plate. Splinter damage can be seen to the port side of the warship's hull and the wooden launch. Note also the burnt-out wreckage of *Graf Spee*'s Arado seaplane. (Historic Military Press)

Top: A view of *Admiral Graf Spee*'s bow taken whilst she was anchored in Montevideo Harbour following the Battle of the River Plate. Note the ship's badge mounted just forward of her anchors and hause pipes, false bow wave camouflage (nick-named 'The Moustache'), and shell damage in the upper hull side (at right). (US Naval Historical Center)

Above: When word spread that *Admiral Graf Spee*'s departure from Montevideo Harbour was imminent on 17 December 1939, thousands gathered along the shoreline to watch, believing they were about to witness a great naval battle. Shortly after 18.00 hours, with a reduced crew of just forty-two men, the warship steamed out of port. (Historic Military Press)

Above: The *Admiral Graf Spee* pictured still burning after being scuttled in the River Plate estuary off Montevideo, Uruguay, on 17 December 1939. (Historic Military Press)

Below: Another view of the burning wreck of *Admiral Graf Spee* in the River Plate estuary off Montevideo. (Historic Military Press)

Top: The Union Flag being waved in Montevideo as a large crowd gather at the waterfront to welcome HMS *Ajax* which had been given permission to dock at Montevideo for twenty-four hours to re-provision following the Battle of River Plate. (Historic Military Press)

Above: The prison ship *Altmark* pictured in Josing Fiord (Jøssingfjord) prior to the Royal Navy's rescue of the seamen incarcerated onboard. (Historic Military Press)

Above: HMS *Achilles* arriving in Auckland on 23 February 1940 following the Battle of the River Plate.

Below: The latest Battle Honour being added to HMS *Ajax*'s carved scroll of honours by the 'Captain of the Quarter Deck', Petty Officer W. Perfitt. (Historic Military Press)

shadowing cruisers, too far away to intervene. The captain of the *Shakespeare* had ideas of his own, however, and they did not include abandoning his ship. He refused to give the order to his crew, and they all stood and watched the German battleship as she swung into position to use her torpedoes.

It was a critical moment. The *Shakespeare*'s crew, as it were, standing their ground; the *Graf Spee* looming up as intimidatingly as possible.

Then the moment passed. Langsdorff suddenly ordered his ship on her old course towards Montevideo, and passed a surprised *Shakespeare* – astonished after all that an enemy should let them go unharmed. Ever afterwards they held a respect for Captain Langsdorff as a man who would not lightly take life even in war. Commodore Harwood's opinion was that this was a ruse to delay pursuit. It didn't come off because the *Shakespeare*'s captain refused to take to his boats.

Shortly after this, Lieutenant Washbourn made a report to *Achilles*' captain that a strange vessel had been sighted in the general line of flight of the *Graf Spee*. At first she had the appearance of a merchantman, but suddenly the look-outs noticed that she had a streamlined funnel and an unusual silhouette. All that Washbourn knew was that from a distance she had the uncomfortable appearance of a man-o'-war, and he knew there was no friendly warship nearer than the Falkland Islands.

Her unusual appearance agreed with recent information received concerning Hitler's new Hipper-class cruisers, and at once these suspicions were called down to Captain Parry. The news brought the *Achilles*' captain on to the bridge immediately, saying, "I think I'll close a little further before reporting, Guns".

After a few minutes of close observation, the matter seemed beyond doubt. Captain Parry decided that here was an Admiral Hipper class cruiser hurrying up to the aid of the

Graf Spee. He ordered Signals to transmit an enemy report: "*Ajax*. Emergency. Enemy in sight."

A startled Commodore Harwood asked for further information, and Captain Parry replied, "Suspected 8-inch cruiser. Am confirming."

There was tension in the two cruisers now as they waited the arrival of a new enemy, herself more powerful than either of them, even without the assistance of the *Graf Spee*. The Battle of the River Plate seemed nowhere near over.

Commodore Harwood immediately ordered *Achilles* not to engage the approaching cruiser; that way lay certain suicide, and it was far better for the two British ships to shadow their formidable enemies in the hope that more powerful reinforcements could ultimately be brought up to engage them. Rather a forlorn hope, considering the wide dispersal of British naval forces at that moment.

Exeter, limping south, received a signal ordering her to keep clear of the coast and warning her of the new enemy.

Every eye aboard the two cruisers turned repeatedly in the next half hour towards the newcomer on the horizon, yet attention was in no way relaxed from the watch on the speeding *Graf Spee*. Tension mounted as the distant ship came slowly over the horizon. ...

Then everyone relaxed, and as relief flowed through them it was as if they had scored another victory.

This was no German battleship. Now they could identify her, a French ship of unusual appearance, the S.S. *Delane*. Innocently she ploughed her way towards the Plate, not realising what alarm she had caused with her streamlined funnel and curious superstructure, unaware that she had blundered on the fringes of a dramatic sea battle.

"*Ajax*," Captain Parry signalled, "False alarm".

Now they could relax. They had only the mighty *Graf Spee* in some way to outwit and defeat. Only ...

As the day wore on, it seemed to become certain that the

German raider's destination was the River Plate, and the *Ajax* repeatedly transmitted warnings to all British merchant ships to keep out of the way. Right to the end, though, no one really believed that the more powerful, comparatively undamaged German would deliberately bottle herself inside the Plate Estuary. Not capable of such abject strategy themselves, the personnel of the British ships uneasily suspected a ruse – something was going to happen shortly, they opined; it was unthinkable that the *Graf Spee* should run from them without further fight.

Yet all that hot afternoon she kept on running, dragging the miles under her until she was sailing in coastal waters. Abruptly, though, the German turned, like an angered beast lashing out at its tormentors, firing two 11-inch salvoes at *Ajax*. The range was about 26,000 yards and the gunnery was good. The first salvo was short but in line. As *Ajax* made a quick turn, the second salvo fell in her wake.

As if discouraged by her failure to surprise the British cruiser, the *Graf Spee* once more resumed her flight westward towards the mouth of the Plate. But now they had an interested spectator of the fight that was beginning to develop again with the coming of darkness,

It was another warship.

Chapter 16

Battle in Uruguayan Territorial Waters

They had heard news of the battle off-shore in Uruguay, and there was great excitement in the port of Montevideo. At 1642 the Uruguayan cruiser, the *Uruguay*, was ordered out to report on the situation off territorial waters. Captain Fernando J. Fuentes and crew were therefore privileged to witness an exciting chase and the final phases of a bitter battle that had started at first light that morning.

At 1814 look-outs on the *Uruguay* sighted a warship approaching which later proved to be the *Graf Spee*. As they watched, they saw the big battleship change course and fire two salvoes into a smoke screen on the horizon. Then she came back on her course and steadily became larger to the watchers as she drew nearer.

The German was flying some signal which could not be understood by the Uruguayans because the fire control tower of the battleship obstructed the view. Captain Fuentes ordered a signal to be made, saying – "I see your signals, but cannot make them out. I assume they are a warning of the existence of a danger zone".

It was an understatement. With the gathering of night, the battle was brewing up again.

According to Captain Fuentes, the remainder of the battle was fought in Uruguayan territorial waters, within the shadow of the coastal hills. Sometimes as close as 3,000 yards to the British cruiser *Ajax*, the report stated, the *Uruguay* kept up with the battle.

With the setting of the sun, the British ships crept closer to their adversary. Now, they felt, was a critical time. If the *Graf Spee* gave them the slip in the darkness, doubling on her tracks and heading for the open sea, they might lose their quarry, after all. Those were the days before radar, and it would probably be impossible to follow the German through the night.

The cruisers opened fire again in an effort to damage further the *Graf Spee* and crowded her towards the bottleneck of the River Plate. The tactics of Commodore Harwood were brilliant.

As the sun set, he ordered both ships to shadow in such a way that the battleship was silhouetted against the setting sun while they remained in the deepening shadows to the east of the *Graf Spee*. Later, as darkness came, they manœuvred so that the raider was caught against the background of bright lights festooning the coast of a country enjoying neutrality in war-time. Shrouded against the deeper darkness farther off-shore, it is doubtful if the *Graf Spee* so much as saw her pursuers after sunset, except for the flash of guns trying to cripple her. *Achilles* even came to within five miles of the battleship as daylight faded, in an effort to hit her and hurt her so that she was beyond any further tricks.

During the run towards the entrance to the River Plate, Langsdorff several times put out smoke screens to give him-self protection against the accurate gunnery of his pursuers. He was also firing his 11-inch guns when he could, doubtless still hoping for a last-minute success, but handicapped because Commodore Harwood was brilliantly dictating the course of battle. Hitting almost unseen targets demanded more luck than Langsdorff was getting, this tragic day of his life.

Achilles, running close in the deep shadows of the Uruguayan coastline, suddenly opened heavy fire on the battleship. The *Graf Spee* replied, perhaps rather desperately because *Achilles* could hardly have been visible, with three 11-inch salvoes. *Achilles* fired five salvoes, reported by *Ajax* to be straddling the German raider.

The *Graf Spee*, well within territorial waters now, fired off further salvoes at 2132, 2140 and 2143, but as Commodore Harwood later reported, the intention was probably merely to keep the New Zealand-manned ship at a respectful distance, for again the target was too obscure to permit of serious shooting.

All this time *Ajax* was shadowing from a point further south, beyond the English Bank, to intercept the *Graf Spee* if at the last minute she tried to duck back and head for the open sea.

But at 0050 on December 14 the fight ended – the fight at sea, but not on land. A weary, battered, discouraged German crew dropped anchor in the Montevideo roads. Across the entrance to the harbour, two cruisers began a ceaseless patrol to make sure the German didn't change her mind and come out in the middle of the night.

She didn't.

Chapter 17

The Diplomatic Battle Begins

The *Graf Spee* was in harbour, but the Battle of the River Plate was nowhere near over. Now began a diplomatic battle coupled with a tremendous bluff and race against time.

It really started in the afternoon of the battle, when first it began to appear as though the *Graf Spee* might be heading towards the River Plate. Commodore Harwood reported the fact to the British Naval Attaché in Montevideo, Captain H.W. McCall.

Next, the Naval Attaché received information that the pocket battleship *was* entering Montevideo, and there was no sleep for the British Legation staff that night.

Hovering anxiously in the darkness of the River Plate, Commodore Harwood's concern was in case the *Graf Spee* might give them the slip in the night: the estuary was wide and two ships could not possibly cover it unaided. Accordingly a signal was despatched to Captain McCall asking for assistance.

The Naval Attaché promptly rounded up a number of tugs and aircraft which he hired to go out on patrol, ready to pass information immediately if the German raider moved from her anchorage. The tugs were to maintain patrol during darkness, and the aircraft were to fly off at dawn and spot the *Graf Spee* if she had in fact eluded the watchers and escaped into the Atlantic again.

There were more signals during the night, hours of the closest co-operation between Commodore Harwood and the British Minister in Montevideo, Mr. E. Millington-Drake. "At all costs the *Graf Spee* must be detained in Montevideo harbour while reinforcements hurry up," was the tenor of Commodore Harwood's signals. Reinforcements – the *Ark Royal, Renown, Neptune, Dorsetshire, Shropshire, Cumberland* and three destroyers – were speeding flat out for the River Plate. Mighty ships, magnificent ships, some of them capable of blowing the pocket battleship clean out of the water if they could only get there in time.

But that was the trouble. They couldn't. The only re-inforcement Harwood could expect was the *Cumberland*, and without disparaging that gallant ship, she was hardly of size to be considered seriously as opposition to a pocket battleship. Effectively she could hope to be no more fortunate than the courageous *Exeter*, and in fact the experts aboard *Ajax* and *Achilles* wrote her off in a similar role – she'd be the target ship, they prophesied, absorbing the fire as *Exeter* had done, in the hope that the smaller cruisers could sneak in and deal damaging blows under cover of the diversion.

All of which did not prevent the *Cumberland* from straining her boilers in an effort to reach the River Plate in time to participate in a possible battle with the German. In fact she made a record trip for a ship of her class, actually reaching the Plate only thirty-four hours after heaving up anchor in the Falkland Islands.

But fast though she was heading north, the *Cumberland* could not arrive before about midnight of December 14. For almost twenty-four hours, only *Achilles* and the battered *Ajax* were between the *Graf Spee* and freedom, if the battleship decided to make a bold dash for the obscurity of the open sea.

Twenty-four hours. "Keep the German inside Montevideo for at least a day at all costs," Commodore Harwood urged, and it provided comedy relief in the battle of tactics ashore.

When the British Minister first received the signal, announcing the *Graf Spee*'s apparent intention to seek shelter in Montevideo, he promptly dashed round to the Uruguayan Foreign Minister, Dr. Guani, and demanded that the German be given no asylum, however temporary. Mr. Millington-Drake at the time thought the *Graf Spee* must have been a severely damaged ship to run before the British cruisers, and did not realise until later that the damage was mostly with the British force. So his tactics in the beginning were to force the German raider to sea before she had time to make any repairs to her armament, and to this end he talked indignantly and at length on the subject, protesting vigorously when the Uruguayans said that by the Rules of International Warfare the warship of a belligerent country was entitled to stay in a neutral harbour for twenty-four hours – if she stayed longer than that, she would be interned. The British interests did not want this – they required the *Graf Spee* to be sunk or captured by the British so that there was no possibility of her somehow escaping from internment to begin her damaging role again.

Ashore in the British Legation they were still trying to upset the Uruguayans' twenty-four-hour decision, when a signal from Harwood told them the horrid truth. The *Graf Spee* had all her armament virtually intact, while only one small sound cruiser could do battle if the German raider came out – one and a half cruisers, as the *Ajax* was quick to point out.

From that moment, the Minister did everything to hold the *Graf Spee* inside Montevideo harbour. True, he maintained the fiction that he wanted the *Graf Spee* to put to sea at once, but this was bluff to add to the Germans' feelings that a big British naval force must be waiting for the battered battleship outside the harbour. McCall took more practical steps to detain the *Graf Spee*, however. When he had rounded up tugs to act as spotters out in the roads, he also summoned to the Legation all the captains of British merchantmen in Montevideo and gave them orders.

Whether ready for sailing or not, one of them must put to sea immediately, he ordered. By the Rules of International Warfare, much quoted in the past hours by all parties, no belligerent warship was allowed to sail from a neutral port within twenty-four hours of the departure of a merchantman of the opposing country. A British ship, the S.S. *Ashworth*, immediately put to sea and at once Mr. Millington-Drake invoked the twenty-four-hour clause. This was accepted at once by the courteous, co-operative Uruguayans. Too co-operative, the German Minister was later to protest; the Uruguayans were not so much neutral, he declared, as demonstrably pro-British. But he could not argue about the twenty-four-hour injunction following the sailing of the British merchantman; that was quite clearly covered in the Rules of International Warfare. Besides, Captain Langsdorff was asking for a long period now in order to make his ship fit for battle again.

The British Minister was informed about the *Graf Spee*'s application for extended time, but did not necessarily feel that it might genuinely be for the purpose of making repairs. He thought it could be bluff, to give the German time to select a moment during a particularly dark night when he might slip away unobserved by the ships across the roads. So he arranged for another merchantman to sail later that day, so that once again he could invoke the twenty-four-hour restraint on sailing rule. He proposed to keep this up and, with the co-operation of the Uruguayans, make sure the *Graf Spee* did not leave harbour.

Chapter 18

The Press Arrive

By this time the world knew of the battle. From Japan to America, New Zealand to Germany, the radio and Press of the world carried versions of the Battle of the River Plate. Few of them were accurate. The Germans, shocked to have to report that one of their much-vaunted pocket battleships had run before smaller British cruisers, gave an account which was vastly different from the British report. Dr. Goebbels, Propaganda Minister for the Reich, screamed that the British had behaved inhumanely towards a solitary warship attacked by a larger fleet.

The British Admiralty report was guarded in some aspects of the battle, but remarkably wide of the truth in others. They inspired the B.B.C. to put out news stories intended to fool the enemy who would undoubtedly hear them. According to the B.B.C., the *Graf Spee* was trapped inside Montevideo, while outside the estuary of the River Plate a mighty British fleet had swiftly gathered, waiting for the raider to come out to her death. Even to this day, that story is still believed by many people all over the world, because afterwards the truth received less prominence than the propaganda following the battle.

In the two cruisers, patiently patrolling across the estuary, the men heard B.B.C. reports of mighty naval reinforcements and promptly rushed up on deck to look them over. Bewildered, they saw nothing larger than a tug keeping watch with them. They shook their heads. The B.B.C. were crackers. There wasn't any mighty fleet off Montevideo, only *Achilles*, and *Ajax* with half her guns out of commission.

But Captain Langsdorff and the German Ambassador believed the broadcast. They had to – the British Consulate made sure of that.

From the United States came crack Press reporters and cameramen to have a close up view of the next stage in the battle they had just missed. They flew in within a matter of hours, and British officials ashore got at them and secured their goodwill and co-operation. In a matter of hours the cables were humming with reports from these reporters of a neutral country. Some said they had flown out far beyond the mouth of the River Plate and graphically described the hungry ships waiting for the unhappy *Graf Spee* to come poking her nose out of the neutral harbour.

Others reported the presence of the *Renown* in nearby Rio de Janeiro – she had up-anchored and was racing south to the River Plate and would be there in time if the German came out to do battle, they wrote.

It was depressing news for Langsdorff, perhaps not be-lieved until his own look-out reported the *Renown* in the English roads. It was a mistake in identification, perhaps engendered by jumpy nerves and an imagination made hypersensitive by the radio reports they were receiving aboard the *Graf Spee*. But Langsdorff himself accepted it, and perhaps it dictated all his later decisions. Now he was truly bottled in, with no great chance of escaping while such a formidable force stood between him and freedom.

But Langsdorff did not seem in a hurry. In fact he appeared to be full of other problems, not the least of them being the need to report to his masters in Berlin. His defeat at sea was going to take some explaining.

Still, whatever the reason, the passing hours gave the *Cumberland* time to race up and join them.

Chapter 19

The Prisoners are Freed

The prisoners aboard the *Graf Spee* fell asleep in their hammocks during the quietness of the night following the battle. After a few hours, while it was still dark, they heard the door being opened and woke up. Lieutenant Hertzberger, one of Langsdorff's officers, came in and spoke to them. They did not understand what he was saying at first, something about: "Gentlemen, you are now free as we are entering Montevideo harbour."

At that moment the engines stopped, and the silence was uncanny. After a few seconds, someone scrambled from his hammock and looked out through the broken skylight. They heard a startled exclamation and then the man called, "It's right. I can see the lights of Monte!" They were in harbour, and though Hertzberger's statement was an anticipation, in a short while they might reasonably expect to taste freedom again.

Delighted, they crowded round Hertzberger, an officer popular with the prisoners. He told them that eight torpedoes had been fired at the *Graf Spee* but all had missed. The officer looked worn out, but managed to smile as he said, "I hope I never again come into contact with the British Navy".

Hertzberger said the Germans were very impressed with the courage of the small cruisers which had come as close as four miles in their attack on the *Graf Spee*. Particularly they were impressed by the resolution of the *Exeter*, which had continued to fight when clearly she was hardly able to do so.

Some of the merchant ships' captains were taken up to say goodbye to Langsdorff, and they found him still smiling but looking very weary and depressed. When Captain Dove of the *Africa Star* came in, Langsdorff said he would like to shake hands with him. He paid a great tribute to the British ships and said their gunnery was magnificent.

In earlier conversations with the British captains, Langsdorff had told them he had been a guest of Admiral Cunningham during the time of the Naval Review off Spithead, and had been presented to the King and Queen. He considered this to be a great honour.

He talked about Hitler and while he did not appear to be too enthusiastic over the dictator personally, he said he thought his advent had been good for Germany. He agreed the Germans did not have much freedom, but he also thought that was good for them, too.

Langsdorff said he had hoped to return to Germany for Christmas, but the sinking of the *Rawalpindi* by the *Deutschland* had made the North Atlantic too hot for an attempt to run home, and he had decided to linger on in the south. He said his crew were only "beggar boys", and he hadn't many good sailors, adding that it had been very difficult in Germany to build up a navy since the First World War. Particularly, he said, it had been difficult to get the right type of officers.

Now, in his last meeting with the captains, he appeared to be upset when he informed them that he was not going to sea with over a thousand men in a ship in her present unseaworthy condition. He said it would be suicide. Captain Dove's opinion was that Langsdorff was a gentleman, in the strictest sense of the word, much too humane for the job he was doing, and he should never have taken it on.

Langsdorff appeared to regret very much that his country was at war with Britain, and said the trouble was that Hitler and Chamberlain had first agreed, then Hitler had learned through his Intelligence in Czechoslovakia something which turned him against Chamberlain and would not let him trust the British Government any further.

He gave Captain Dove a cap with *Graf Spee* ribbons as a souvenir, and then the prisoners went back to their quarters to wait for release.

But time went by and the men began to be restless as no one seemed to take any notice of them in their captivity. The crew of the *Graf Spee* were hard at work painting her and repairing the damage. Some food was brought after dawn, but it was little, and anyway they wanted freedom and not more black bread. It was explained to them that it was impossible to cook food, and the crew were receiving the same rations. The courteous Captain Langsdorff sent an apology for the poor fare.

Afternoon came, and still they were held prisoners, even though they were in a neutral harbour. They were not to know – though they probably guessed – what frantic efforts were being made to secure their release by the British officials in Montevideo. What they were afraid of was that the German ship might suddenly make a dash for the harbour entrance and carry them away with her.

About five o'clock, just when hope had almost died away, an officer came and ordered them to be ready to leave the ship in half an hour. They were all ready, and had been for hours, and the last half-hour seemed interminable.

Then again the door opened, and a smiling German officer led them to where a tug waited alongside. It was a glorious moment for the men, some of whom had been prisoners for sixty-five days. Ashore, having passed through Immigration, they were handed over to the British Consular staff. A great crowd of Uruguayans was awaiting them and gave them a magnificent reception. They were different with the Germans, however, abusing them and calling them cowards.

Thirty-seven men had been killed aboard the *Graf Spee* in the action, and fifty-seven were more or less seriously wounded.

As soon as daylight came, the German crew got to work on the damage. It was more extensive than the British had realised; their gunnery had been excellent and they had scored between sixty and seventy hits. Now much wreckage had to be cleared away, electric leads repaired, shell-holes plugged, and the ship brought as near as possible to its former state of efficiency. But the crew, tired after their unusual ordeal, demoralised by having to run before an enemy which in theory should have run before them, worked without spirit.

Dr. Otto Langmann, the German Minister at Montevideo, came aboard before daylight, a stout man with a pince-nez, much disliked in Uruguay. His first statement to Captain Langsdorff was in effect a reproof. Langsdorff had come to the wrong port for shelter, he declared.

This was startling to a sailor with perhaps little idea of politics, but Langmann told him how pro-British Uruguay was, and how much better it would have been if he had brought the *Graf Spee* into the Argentine port of Buenos Aires – Argentina, Fascist on the lines of Germany and Italy and sympathetic towards the totalitarian states. Britain would exert all her efforts to make Uruguay obey her wishes, Langmann declared nastily. But all the annoyance with Langsdorff was wasted because now there was no changing the decision; the *Graf Spee* was inside Montevideo harbour, and could not easily get out of it.

Then the German Naval Attaché at Buenos Aires flew in. He brought with him German civilian constructors to help repair the ship, and it was just as well because to date all Uruguayan firms had steadfastly refused to make the *Graf Spee* ready for sea.

When the German constructors saw the damage, they immediately declared it impossible to effect repairs in less than fourteen days. Dr. Langmann promptly applied for fourteen days' grace to stay in Montevideo harbour. It is still not certain what the German tactics were, but believing they were bottled in now by superior forces, unwilling to be interned for the duration of the war, perhaps they played for time in the hope that something would turn up to their advantage.

One theory was that if only the *Graf Spee* could hold the attention long enough, Hitler would hurry up submarines to harry the supposed British naval forces offshore. In all the confusion the *Graf Spee* might, on a dark night, escape. Whatever the reason, the Germans most truculently demanded fourteen days' stay. Without quite knowing why the Germans did it, the British Minister promptly protested against it, and the Uruguayans, caught between two sides, compromised by granting seventy-two hours' stay, following an inspection by their own naval experts. The seventy-two hours did not commence, incidentally, until after the inspection, so that all in all the *Graf Spee*'s time in Montevideo would in fact extend to over ninety hours.

On Friday, December 15th, with the *Cumberland* now on patrol with *Achilles* and *Ajax*, the R.F.A. *Olynthus* (Captain L.N. Hill) came out to refuel the last-named cruisers. The weather was not good, and heavy seas soon put an end to the operation after *Ajax* had taken aboard only two hundred tons of oil. The position so far as fuel was concerned was not too happy for the British ships, all being very low on oil after the long journeys of recent days. In fact, if the *Graf Spee* came out and kept going long enough, lack of fuel would cause the British cruisers to have to give up the chase.

In Montevideo, the *Graf Spee* had been refuelled at frantic pace in the first hours in harbour, from the German supply ship waiting there, the *Tacoma*. She could have gone to sea at any time, but Langsdorff was making no bold dashes for freedom. He was in touch with Grand Admiral Raeder in Berlin, and all his subsequent actions appear to have been dictated from the German Admiralty.

At the time, the world was thrilled by Press accounts which said that Hitler had personally telephoned Langsdorff in South America. This was probably incorrect, but the World-Against-Hitler was regaled with stories of violent abuse from the Führer because Langsdorff had been driven into seeking shelter by a weaker force. Germany had lost an enormous amount of face by the action and no hysterical propaganda could detract from the British victory. Langsdorff's courteous and humane treatment of his victims had been fully detailed by Press and radio, and he was a very respected and even popular enemy. Certainly he held the British and American sympathies in the reported altercation with his master, for Langsdorff was manifestly a gentleman, and Hitler most certainly was not.

In between conferences with German officials, meetings with Uruguayans and inspections of damages to be repaired, Langsdorff had one more melancholy duty, on December 15, when the Germans had to bury their dead.

Here was an opportunity for propaganda in a neutral country, and the Germans (probably the politician, Dr. Langmann, rather than the sailor, Captain Langsdorff) freely availed themselves of the moment. Permission was asked of the Uruguayan authorities for the burial of the German dead ashore with full military honours. The Uruguayans without hesitation granted the request.

The burial was the subject of an almost world-wide radio hook-up, with commentators from most countries giving their impressions of the melancholy ceremony. The Press were there, too, and within a matter of hours photographs of the event were printed in the principal newspapers in Europe and

America. Newsreel photographers shot thousands of feet of film, to be flown all over the world within a matter of hours.

At times, it was more like a circus than the funeral of young men violently done to death in the interests of a power-crazy megalomaniac. The brass band of the *Graf Spee* led the cortège through the streets of Montevideo, jammed with spectators. Behind marched Langsdorff with a large and very smart contingent from his crew.

Among the crowd were many Germans and some German sympathisers, who made the Nazi salute as the funeral procession slowly passed by. But most Uruguayans, while respectful of the dead, were less in sympathy with the Germans than with the popular British. However, without any unfortunate incident to mar the proceedings, the ceremony of interment was performed.

Captain Langsdorff, white uniformed, bemedalled and with the Nazi Eagle emblem on his right breast, deliverer a brief funeral ovation over the coffins. Photographs show him standing over them, with their Nazi flag coverings, a man hollow-eyed and haggard. Around him were several German civilians, including the pince-nezed Dr. Langmann.

The newsreel cameramen captured for the world of propaganda an interesting moment almost at the end of the ceremony. Captain Langsdorff sprinkled earth over each coffin before it was lowered out of sight of the huge crowd that had pressed into the cemetery. That done, the Germans came to a stiff attention, preparatory to a salute to the departed.

Every hand came up in a Nazi salute – except one.

Captain Langsdorff's hand swept up into a correct naval salute.

It must have been upsetting to the German propagandists, that the well-respected Langsdorff in this final moment of tribute to the dead, should have rejected the Nazi salute in favour of the traditional one. To many it seemed like a rejection of Nazism, too, and the Press in Britain and America were not slow to enlarge upon the theory. In pictures of the ceremony, the German Minister can be seen looking hard at Langsdorff holding his salute, his expression promising trouble for the captain when there were no spectators. Probably it came, but if so there is no record of what was said between them. Langsdorff, in any event, could hardly have cared about Nazi ambassadors; for by now it is possible he had determined his own fate.

Propagandists on both sides unscrupulously used the funeral to hurt their enemies. Berlin seethed with fury against the British when a report was issued that British seamen, released from the *Graf Spee*, had spat upon the graves of the dead and thrown the corpse of a dog upon a coffin.

In fact some of the former prisoners, including all the captains of captured British merchantmen, attended the funeral and they subscribed to buy a wreath which bore the inscription: "To the memory of the brave men of the sea, from their comrades of the British Merchant Service." War being war, this was not quoted to the German people and they continued to believe the worst about the ex-PoWs.

In turn, reports were issued that some of the coffins did not contain corpses but small arms and ammunition, to be dug up for use by the German Fifth Column in Montevideo. Again there is no evidence that this was true.

Chapter 20

A Propaganda War

Ashore, the diplomats fought their battles, while the grey wolfish shapes of the British cruisers prowled across the Plate estuary and kept the unhappy Langsdorff in harbour. But on the air a fierce propaganda battle was being waged, with charge and denial being flung from one warring nation to another. In Germany, desperate efforts were being made to convince the people not only that the Battle of the River Plate was a German victory, but that her opponents had behaved in a despicable and outrageous manner.

Victory, claimed the German News Agency, was the Fatherland's because both the *Achilles* and *Exeter* had been sunk, and the *Ajax* had run away. The *Graf Spee*, without injury, had sailed into Montevideo to take in fresh supplies and refuel. Germany rang with the news, and victory celebrations were held.

Even twenty-four hours later, when the truth must have been known to Ribbentrop and Goebbels, the lie was continued so far as the German people were concerned, though this time there were subtle differences.

Issued at 1315 G.M.T., December 14, was the following report by the German News Agency: "For three and a half months German warships have been cruising on the high seas. During this period they have inflicted the most serious damage to British shipping and have cornered British ships wherever they have met them. It will be possible at a later date to divulge the real measure of the great successes achieved by the German cruisers."

Cruisers, they were beginning to call the pocket battleships. ...

"The British have been continuously hunting the German ships, but owing to the superior sea strategy of the Germans, were unable to register the slightest success. According to messages from Montevideo, the *Graf Spee* on Wednesday towards six o'clock in the morning, came across three British cruisers, *Exeter*, *Achilles* and *Ajax*, at a point about twenty miles east of Punta del Este in front of the La Plata estuary, which hitherto had been regarded as the uncontested sphere of the British Atlantic Fleet.

"The German battleship immediately opened fire. The roaring of the guns could clearly be heard at a coastal holiday resort fifty miles distant from the battle-ground. ... Later the cruiser *Exeter* was seen to be shot to pieces by the heavy salvoes of the *Graf Spee*, and the British cruiser *Ajax* fled. Soon the superstructure of the *Exeter* resembled merely a chaotic tangle of twisted steel and iron girders. The bridge was equally swept away . . . more salvoes of the *Graf Spee* forced the British cruiser to turn away and to drop out of the fight.

"The battle ended in the victory of the *Graf Spee*, which in the evening entered the La Plata estuary and anchored in the harbour of Montevideo. She had not only forced the *Exeter* to abandon the battle but had also registered severe hits on the *Achilles* and the *Ajax*. The *Graf Spee* was hit by only a few shells.

"According to unconfirmed reports from the harbour police, the *Graf Spee* has several dead and wounded on board, while there are hundreds of dead and wounded on the British ships."

Then came the lie that was to bring Germany seething with indignation at the cowardly British opponents.

"It became known that the British in breach of international law fired gas shells at the *Graf Spee*, and in particular mustard gas was used ... among the wounded are a number of cases of gas poisoning."

Mustard gas, a weapon to fill people illogically with horror – a lie told early on to capture the sympathy of the masses so that they would not notice the changes that would have to come in the later German news reports on the battle.

Dr. Langmann, the German Minister in Montevideo, made the first allegations that mustard gas had been employed after he had visited the *Graf Spee* early on December 14. He alleged that the majority of the wounded German sailors were suffering from injuries inflicted by gas bombs, including several suffering from eye injuries.

Now the German News Agency was cleverly making use of the allegation that mustard gas had been used against the German ship. A weak point about their communiqué had been the statement that the *Graf Spee* had disposed of her opponents and then run into harbour. Why? puzzled Germans might ask. If the British had been disposed of, why not continue the cruise at sea?

"As a consequence of the use of gas there was the risk of the food stores on the *Admiral Graf Spee* being contaminated, and the commander decided to put into the La Plata river in order to change the food stores."

The same report said that the latest information was that the *Exeter* was lying crippled outside the mouth of the La Plata river, waiting to be towed away, while "unconfirmed reports (state) the British cruiser *Achilles* is sunk". It also spoke of "the effect the victory had had on the American nation, and how tens of thousands of people in Montevideo were loudly voicing their admiration for the heroic battle fought by one solitary warship against at least three British".

... at least three British. They were paving the way for an acceptable announcement of something approaching defeat.

This positive statement about the destruction of the *Exeter* and the sinking of the *Achilles* was flashed round the world and caused distress in the Empire where it was sometimes believed. However, a puzzled American, broadcasting from Berlin, could find several flaws in the communiqué, not the least being – why on earth should the British have employed mustard gas shells against an armour-plated battleship? It was a story to satisfy the German civilians, but could hardly impress experienced sailors.

Nevertheless, for hours and even days the Germans shrilly trumpeted their charges involving the use of mustard gas. How the story of mustard gas poisoning began is not clear, but one statement is that the deception started when a German doctor went on board the *Graf Spee* the first morning in Montevideo with Dr. Langmann. The dead had been laid out on the quarter deck of the ship, and again sprayed with strong disinfectant. The German doctor at once declared the disinfectant to be mustard gas, and the lie, hatched, took on immediate if unpleasant lie.

To clear up the matter, a committee of distinguished medical men in Uruguay was called upon by the Government to examine the dead and injured. The leading surgeon of Montevideo was on this committee, a Dr. Walter Meerhoff, who was of German descent. The charge was unanimously rejected by the committee but, truth being vulnerable in wartime, this proved no deterrent to Dr. Goebbels.

The lie about the use of mustard gas was developed. On December 16, the German News Agency released the following statement, in conflict with all neutral reports at the time: "The well-known Uruguayan eye-specialist, Professor Dr. Walter Meerhoff, received a telegram from the English newspaper, *News-Chronicle*, asking him, as a neutral medical authority, to examine the alleged gas poisoning of the sailors of the German cruiser, *Admiral Graf Spee*. ... Dr. Meerhoff established beyond question the presence of typical symptoms of mustard gas injuries. ... Dr. Meerhoff cabled his findings to the *News-Chronicle*."

Days later Berlin was sticking to its charges that mustard gas had been used, but by this time they were talking to themselves. The end had come to the Battle of the River Plate.

The Berlin radio knew it was coming, and again the news was gradually twisted to be acceptable to a propaganda-drunk public. First they made the supposed victory more impressive: "It is reliably reported that British aircraft also took part in the sea-battle. In the course of the battle several British reconnoitring planes were destroyed by the tremendous blast of the *Graf Spee*'s shells. The heavy British losses are confirmed by the statements made by numerous creditable witnesses."

Then Berlin began to show what sort of opponents her gallant sailors had taken on. The British were quite inhuman and unfit to associate with *Herrenvolk*.

The German News Agency, also on December 16, reported that the *Exeter* "has succeeded in baling out part of the water in her holds, and with the help of the tides has managed to free herself. ... Although two hundred beds for the seriously wounded have already been put in readiness (in Buenos Aires) the British cruiser is said to have suffered to such an extent that apparently she wishes to avoid putting into an Argentine port and prefers to make for the Falkland Islands."

This theme was developed on Sunday, December 17. It told how medical assistance had been taken to the *Exeter*'s injured in far-away Falkland, instead of bringing the wounded to the British doctors and nurses. Four doctors, ten nurses, seven ambulance cars and ten litres of blood had been taken from Buenos Aires to the Falkland Islands, together with 180 beds.

"These facts have caused great astonishment in Argentine circles," the propaganda exclaimed. "It is pointed out that apparently more than 150 gravely wounded of the *Exeter* are made to suffer the painful voyage of several days on the slowly moving and heavily listing cruiser merely in order to prevent the native population of some Argentine port from seeing the badly battered British ship even from afar. Such an attitude is thought clearly inhuman, as owing to the delayed medical attention the number of deaths on board *Exeter* is bound to increase quite unnecessarily."

In another important way, the tune was changing. At first Berlin trumpeted about a noble victory, with the *Graf Spee* emerging scarcely hurt. But within days the German mouthpieces were telling of the overwhelming forces that had fought the *Graf Spee*, and while the latter had secured eventual victory, she was now lying in Montevideo so severely hurt that she needed at least fifteen days to make her ready for sea again. A remarkable *volte face*, and possible only to propagandists.

Germany became abusive towards Uruguay at this point. The South American state was showing bias towards the British, Germany protested. Uruguay was forcing a crippled warship to leave port when she was in no condition to defend herself, whilst outside the harbour was a mighty gathering of British naval power.

Berlin was preparing her people to accept a shock when it came – Admiral Raeder and Hitler had made a terrible decision so far as the end of the *Graf Spee* was concerned.

While the propagandists of both sides sought to make it a victory for their respective countries, three ships maintained a long and anxious vigil across the broad estuary of the River Plate. With the arrival of the *Cumberland*, the situation became somewhat eased for Commodore Harwood, because now he had three ships to patrol the three deep water channels that led out from Montevideo harbour. On December 15 the *Olynthus* also managed to refuel the cruisers, and after that Harwood could breathe freely. Now he could fight and chase the German if the *Graf Spee* came out.

It was monotonous, though, the constant patrol across the roads leading into Montevideo harbour. As day followed day the men on the cruisers grew impatient and only wished the German would come out and finish off the battle one way or another.

But Langsdorff wouldn't come out, or perhaps now his orders from Berlin wouldn't let him come out. Just visible during daylight hours were the patrolling British cruisers, grim, grey ships that dared him to come out and fight – but promised a thrashing if he did so. German Intelligence was bad, and report after report came through of a great gathering of ships in the River Plate. After both the *Ark Royal* and the *Renown* were positively identified by the *Graf Spee*'s gunnery officer as being with the patrolling cruisers, the situation must have seemed beyond possible hope to Langsdorff and the German Minister. How an experienced officer could make such a mistake is not known, and yet the fact is he did.

On Saturday, December 16, there was a scare for the waiting British cruisers. *Ajax* catapulted off her aircraft on a reconnaissance over the harbour of Montevideo. The pilot was instructed to make his survey outside territorial waters. When he returned at 0830 it was to report ominous tidings. He had not been able to sight the *Graf Spee* because of bad visibility, but while flying in the vicinity of the Whistle Buoy suddenly he had been fired upon from below.

At once on board the British cruisers it was assumed that the *Graf Spee* had moved from her moorings and was attempting to escape, and there was excitement aboard the British ships until a report came from Montevideo that the *Graf Spee* was in fact still in harbour. Later it was decided that the firing had come from the Argentine guard gunboat, stationed at Recalada.

About this time Commodore Harwood received a signal from the Admiralty warning him against engaging the *Graf Spee* within the three-mile limit of Uruguayan waters.

Commodore Harwood therefore moved his patrol so as not to infringe territorial rights if it came to battle. One of his problems was the possibility of "overs" landing in Montevideo if a fight did start in the estuary. Altogether the three cruisers had quite a problem in selecting a site for battle which would not widen the patrol area and so enable the German to slip past them undetected.

Still keeping up the gigantic bluff that was hoaxing the Germans, suddenly the B.B.C. broadcast a warning of enemy submarines heading for the River Plate, and immediately the Admiralty ordered mythical destroyers to dash up to the defence of the mythical big ships waiting impatiently for the German raider to creep out.

Berlin was quite satisfied that British battleships, and possibly a couple of French warships, were in the River Plate area now. So much so that Captain Langsdorff received an order to photograph the supposed *Ark Royal*, if at all possible, because a puzzled German Admiralty were genuinely convinced that it had been sunk. The Germans, however, were unable to charter an aircraft for this purpose. In view of the fact that the British had been able to charter aircraft, the refusal to help the Germans is significant of the Uruguayans' friendliness towards the British cause.

In Berlin, Hitler and Raeder were in conference, deciding the *Graf Spee*'s fate. Raeder informed Hitler that Captain Langsdorff wanted to fight his way out of Montevideo harbour and across to the more friendly atmosphere of Buenos Aires, just across the River Plate estuary. Hitler was opposed to any action which could lead to the internment of the battleship, and the *Graf Spee* would certainly be interned if she remained in harbour when the seventy-two hours time limit expired on December 17.

Raeder pointed out the difficulties of the battleship being able to fight her way even the comparatively short distance from Montevideo to Buenos Aires, for he firmly believed in the reports of the concentration of British battleships in the estuary now. The alternative was scuttling.

Hitler's decision was that if the *Graf Spee* stood no chance against the British forces, then Langsdorff should scuttle his ship. Hitler's decision was not out of consideration for men who might lose their lives in an abortive action, but purely political. If he could not gain a victory, he would deny his enemies the right to claim they had made one. Scuttling the *Graf Spee* would in a way cheat the tough British sailors of their prize, and his propagandists would be able to make some capital where they could make none if the German ship were sunk in action.

But Langsdorff did not want to scuttle his ship, and his men now worked desperately under his command to make the raider seaworthy. Ashore, excitement grew to fever pitch as they saw the obvious preparations for a resumption of battle. Tens of thousands of people had flocked into the town, and it was impossible, after a few hours, to find hotel room or other accommodation. Hundreds of thousands of eyes were turned continually upon the grey German battleship with the men working in frantic haste upon her; the harbour area was jammed solid with spectators waiting for the moment when the *Graf Spee* would attempt to break out – hoping to have a grandstand view of a naval battle right outside Montevideo harbour. Little work was done in the Uruguayan capital in the days while she lay in harbour. Little else was discussed save the battleship and the imminent battle expected by the excited populace.

It seems possible that Langsdorff, in spite of pressure from Berlin, was going to pick his moment and make a run for it to Buenos Aires. But then came disaster to his plans. The British Naval Attaché ordered another merchant ship, the S.S. *Dunster Grange*, to sail. The ship left Montevideo at 1700 on December 16. Promptly the British Minister lodged an injunction restraining the German battleship from leaving port within the next twenty-four hours.

It was cunningly done. It meant that Langsdorff could not pick his time to slip away, perhaps during the darkness of the morning of the 17th, but now must leave in daylight. Again the British were dictating the terms of battle.

The sailing of the *Dunster Grange* was a terrible blow to Langsdorff, because it meant that now officially he could not leave Montevideo before 1815 on the 17th. As his time limit to escape internment expired at 2000 the same day it gave him less than two hours in which to quit port. It also meant that he would have to leave harbour in daylight, too, and that must have been a depressing prospect.

In fact, to Langsdorff it must have seemed the end.

It is difficult now to realise what intense excitement was concentrated in the South American port during those few hectic days while Langsdorff made his decisions. To millions of people all over the world it seemed inevitable there must be a sea battle and it would be fought before an enormous grandstand of South American citizens.

By now every radio corporation in America, and those of other countries, had their on-the-spot commentators giving hour by hour descriptions of events as the tension mounted. Programmes all over the world were interrupted as fresh items of news came in.

It is interesting to look back and realise how little were the commentators affected by the German news propaganda. The German version seems to have been healthily disbelieved, and the American commentators especially struck out on a vigorous line of their own which was much nearer to the truth.

As early as the 14th the Associated Press of America had discarded the German story and were broadcasting: "After a furious 14-hour sea duel with three British warships, the Nazi crack 10,000 ton pocket battleship, *Admiral Graf Spee*, today lies trapped and battered in Montevideo harbour."

United Press of America also accurately stated the dead and wounded on the *Graf Spee*: "There are now stated to be 36 dead and 60 wounded on board the German warship. Seven ambulances started removing the injured early this morning."

Their observers down in the harbour area also refuted the first German claims that the *Graf Spee* had suffered little damage. Associated Press released a hand-out on the 14th stating positively: "The *Graf Spee* showed three gaping holes, one at stern and another at forecastle." While the United Press stated baldly, "The *Graf Spee* walked into a trap and then tried to flee out of it".

Later the United Press reported: "An inspection of the exterior of the *Graf Spee* reveals damage so serious that she may be unable to proceed to sea under her own power.

"The sides of the *Graf Spee* have been pierced at least seven times, and part of the superstructure has been shot away. Judging from what one can see of the outside of the *Graf Spee*, it appears that she is probably seriously damaged internally."

After this, of course, the German version changed, and they began to pile on the agony. Where before they had stated that the damage had all been done to the British cruisers, now they were making out that the *Graf Spee* had taken a severe battering and was not fit to be ordered to sea.

The New York *World Telegram* came out with a headline which summarised the situation: "The British set death-watch on *Spee*."

While the New York *Sun* commented: "It is a major irony that the first real naval engagement of the war should have taken place within the 'safety zone.' The fight did violence to the theory that the German pocket battleships are safe from all except a handful of Allied war vessels. If the German vessel intended this engagement, it will be put down as a signal British victory. Naval experts will need to revise their opinions of pocket battleships."

While the crowds gathered, the Press of the world also examined and then discarded the German propaganda that mustard gas had been used by the British. On the 15th, Associated Press released the following statement: "The *Admiral Graf Spee*'s 62 British captives today emphatically denied German charges that the pocket battleship attackers had hurled mustard gas shells at her, and offered themselves as living proofs of this statement. One of the six merchant captains declared: 'During the entire fight the German sailors wore gas masks but we had none.'"

On December 16 both the United Press and Associated Press of America issued a story which ran as follows: "German ships coming? Many rumours that units of the German fleet, including ocean-going submarines, may try to reach the River Plate before the *Graf Spee* sails are circulating in Montevideo. German quarters refuse to make any comment on these rumours."

Perhaps in this report is the reason why the Germans were playing for time. If they had been given fourteen days in which to remain in Montevideo harbour, anything could have happened.

But towards the end of the *Graf Spee*'s stay in Montevideo, the commentators stopped bothering about the German News Agency reports. By now their public wanted to know what fate had been decided for the pocket battleship. The reporters speculated and often were very near the truth.

Typical of the reports are the following:-

United Press: "Zero hour for the departure of the *Admiral Graf Spee* is eight p.m. Montevideo time. There is nothing whatever to indicate whether the warship will submit to internment or make a dash for the ocean."

A later U.P. report added to the first: "As the time limit for the *Graf Spee*'s departure approached, authorised German sources professed to be without information on what orders had been sent to the warship, but their opinion was that she was unlikely to submit to internment."

However, sensationally, later that night, U.P. quoted the semi-official newspaper *El Pueblo*, which reported that Captain Langsdorff said before sailing, "If I cannot get through the naval blockade, I'll sink my ship at 8p.m."

But that is all anticipating the events. For the weary but patient British crews, patrolling wolfishly across the harbour entrance and hoping now for the *Graf Spee* to come out fighting, there was a heartening fillip to their morale.

Chapter 21
Sail for Argentina?

At 1717, December 16, a signal came to Commodore Harwood from the First Lord of the Admiralty, Mr. Winston Churchill. It informed him that he had been appointed by great pleasure of His Majesty a Knight Commander of the Most Honourable Order of the Bath, and that Captains Parry, Woodhouse and Bell were appointed Companions of the same Order. From December 13, 1939, Commodore Harwood had been promoted to be Rear-Admiral in His Majesty's Fleet.

Britain and the Empire had been overjoyed at this first victory over the old enemy, and particularly they had been delighted by the traditional Navy courage in the face of superior odds. The awards, then, were but a symbol of a nation's regard to brave and resolute men.

Rear-Admiral Sir Henry Harwood Harwood immediately made known the awards to the ships in his command, together with yet another signal from the First Sea Lord, saying: "Their Lordships desire to express to you, the captain, officers and ship's company of H.M. ships *Ajax*, *Achilles* and *Exeter*, their highest appreciation of the spirit and determined manner in which the action against the *Admiral Graf Spee* was conducted."

Morale aboard the British cruisers was at its highest in those final hours when Langsdorff had to make a decision between a fight to the death and scuttling his fine ship.

On the *Graf Spee* morale among his youthful crew must have been as low as it could go.

Just before the time came for him to sail or be interned, Langsdorff held a final conference with his senior officers and the German Naval Attaché in Montevideo. At considerable length they discussed their alternatives.

Langsdorff informed them that Dr. Langmann's desperate attempts to give an extension to their time had failed. Uruguay was adamant. In spite of Langmann's pleas that the *Graf Spee* was too unseaworthy to leave harbour, he was informed that if the battleship did not leave by 2000 it would force Uruguay to intern the ship for the duration of war.

Hitler had said there must be no internment.

Langsdorff said to his officers that the time given to him was insufficient for them to patch up their ship – they needed more time, he insisted. One of his officers there-upon remarked, "Why don't we make time, then?"

The *Graf Spee*, after all, was formidable in armament, and the damage it could do to Montevideo if attacked was enormous. More than the speaker felt that the Uruguayans might protest, but could do little if Langsdorff bluntly stated his intention of staying on.

But Langsdorff would not listen to such propositions. He said: "If we stay here and defy the Uruguayans, I am afraid the British ships will come in and get us." Which was probably true.

Langsdorff knew, in any event, better than to rupture international relationships. Uruguay might be a small and comparatively defenceless country, but she was part of America, and Americans were determined to protect each other in case of war. President Roosevelt had already announced his intention of sending powerful naval forces south to Montevideo to protect Uruguay if she felt she was being intimidated.

The last-hour conference dragged on hopelessly.

Internment was out. Staying in harbour was out. Now his experts were dubious about their chances if they tried to make a dash, for Buenos Aires. There was the problem of the very shallow waters in which they would have to navigate. The cooling water intakes might get blocked up, in which event the engines would run hot and possibly seize. The prospect of being a sitting target under the guns of a powerful enemy was not to be contemplated lightly. What advantage, now came the question, was there in fighting across to Buenos Aires, anyway? Friendlier though she might be, Argentina would have to stick to the laws governing the conduct of a neutral nation in time of war. The *Graf Spee* would not be allowed to stay on indefinitely; she would have to sail sometime, and whatever the time they could be sure the British Navy would be out there, waiting for them.

The main argument against further fighting, however, was that no one really felt they would remain long afloat if this time they came within range of enemy guns. There were so many ships out there, they told each other. The *Renown, Ark Royal, Cumberland,* and other mighty ships were crowding round the entrance to the River Plate, just waiting for them. ...

Just waiting for them, in fact, were the *Cumberland*, the *Achilles* and the *Ajax* with only a few of her guns in action. Admiral Harwood said afterwards the odds were with Langsdorff if he had decided to make a night break of it. He rated the British chances of interception as about 30 per cent only.

But British propaganda, not always worthy of credit, this time had completely outbluffed an enemy supposedly expert in winning a war with words.

Chapter 22

Hysteria Ashore

The last hours before the possibility of internment created an atmosphere of tension aboard the three patrolling cruisers and in the British Legation offices ashore. Agents down in the harbour kept the closest watch upon the pocket battleship and reported every move calculated to give an indication of Langsdorff's intentions; these reports were in turn radioed by the Naval Attaché to Admiral Harwood.

First reports to Admiral Harwood on the morning of Sunday, December 17, told of the transfer of welding apparatus and other heavy equipment from the *Graf Spee* to the shore. The officers and men aboard the British cruisers interpreted this as meaning that the *Graf Spee* was going to come out fighting. Now the tension aboard the patrolling ships was almost unbearable as they waited and watched. For if it came to a savage, final fight, however gallantly they fought, and in spite of the arrival of the *Cumberland*, the fact remained they were cruisers matched against one of the most powerful battleships in the world.

The next report swiftly relayed from Montevideo to the ships (but also transmitted by excited radio commentators to an American public) said that between three hundred and four hundred men had left the *Graf Spee* and had transferred to the German supply ship, *Tacoma*, lying close to her.

Later this was to give rise to stories that Langsdorff's young crew had revolted against a further fight, their nerves shattered by the ferocity of the British cruisers' earlier attack. It was proclaimed that this revolt had in fact dictated Langsdorff's final course of action. The British Press at the time played up this angle – all things are fair in wartime, and propagandists are least anxious to know the truth. But no report of Langsdorff mentions such a revolt, and it can be considered as conjectural rather than actual.

At 1720, almost the *Graf Spee*'s deadline, another signal reached the British naval commander. The German raider had transferred another seven hundred men with baggage to the *Tacoma*.

The interpretation of this news by Admiral Harwood was that the *Graf Spee* intended to scuttle herself. He immediately ordered his squadron to close in on the Whistle Buoy, and the three cruisers began to tear in towards Montevideo at 25 knots. Harwood was going to try to board the *Graf Spee* before she had time to go to the bottom. The capture of an abandoned enemy battleship would have meant the final discomfiture of an embarrassed enemy, for Goebbels could hardly have explained that one away.

Langsdorff now informed the harbourmaster that he would sail at 1815, and within minutes the whole city knew his decision, as well as the crews aboard the British cruisers, now closing in rapidly.

By this time the harbour area was solid with spectators excited beyond anything they had ever known before. The radio commentators gabbled without cease, detailing every-thing of significance or without significance in an effort to add to the excitement. The broadcasts were now being received aboard the cruisers and proved just as interesting to the British sailors as they waited at Action Stations.

Shortly after Langsdorff's announcement of his sailing time, a large Nazi ensign was broken out from the *Graf Spee*'s foremast. Seconds later, another flew out from the mainmast.

The hysteria ashore was getting out of hand as slowly one anchor came up, and now for certain they knew she was going out to meet her enemies.

A second anchor came up with apparent reluctance, dripping from the bed of the harbour, and then, imperceptibly at first, the mighty battleship began to move. Now the crowd was silent, watching – knowing that aboard was a gallant captain and no more than sixty officers and men. Was it true, they wondered, that a few men had volunteered with their captain to fight to the death and go down with the ship, as rumour reported?

Stated later to be three-quarters of a million in number, the crowd saw Langsdorff take his ship out of harbour unaided by tugs. Ahead of her were two tugs and a barge from Buenos Aires, which kept their pace with the battleship, causing much speculation from the crowd. Then the *Tacoma* was seen to up anchor and proceed after the battleship.

There *was* going to be a battle, of that the enormous crowd was now certain. Just as certain were the radio commentators, their talk bordering on the hysterical as they told the listening millions all over the world about the approaching fight. The battered but still capable *Graf Spee* was moving out to where three British cruisers could be seen racing in to meet her. The moment was too much for many, and the newspapers the following day told of hundreds of people fainting, of some unfortunates whose hearts could not stand the strain, and of people being injured as the great crowd pushed and swayed to get a better view of the climax to days of suspense and uncertainty.

Distantly an aircraft droned. It was British, the crowd swiftly told each other. But it made no attempt to come inside territorial waters and attack. Harwood's orders to the pilot of the *Ajax*'s plane were to observe and to report – especially to report if the *Graf Spee*'s appearance of being about to scuttle herself were only a ruse … which would be indicated if she suddenly took aboard again her personnel from the *Tacoma*.

The pilot's reports came swiftly back to the crews of the three British ships. First, that the *Graf Spee* was heading straight towards them, followed by her retinue of tugs, barge and *Tacoma* in attendance. That was what they had been expecting, perhaps hoping for. The cruisers maintained their course towards the approaching battleship. ...

From the aircraft, a report: "The *Spee* has changed course. She's heading west, towards the Buenos Aires channel."

At once the situation changed. The *Graf Spee* wasn't going to fight, wasn't going to scuttle herself. She was going to make a run for it to another and possibly more friendly harbour. ...

But she wasn't going to run for it. Shortly after setting on her new course, she was seen to lose speed and finally stop. From a distance, only the circling British aircraft, able to see closely and clearly what was happening, saw the two Argentine tugs and the barge come alongside the German raider.

After all, the ship was to die, and die by the hands of her master.

Chapter 23

Graf Spee is Scuttled

Leaving only the scuttling party to do their work, the remainder of the *Graf Spee*'s crew clambered aboard the barge flying the Argentine flag. When that operation was completed, the barge drew away.

The sun was setting as the drama drew towards its close. Aboard the great German battleship men worked industriously to blow the bottom out of her and start a fire that would gut her and make her worthless to anyone else.

It must have been a depressing, unhappy moment for the men who had lived in her, and who had for her the affection which comes to most men for most ships. To destroy her, to hurt her – to make a useless hulk of a beautiful and seemingly living thing. That was what they had to do upon the orders of their captain.

And Langsdorff. … What must his thoughts have been in that terrible moment before the end of his ship, the ship he had been so proud to command? They must have been bitter, especially bitter because his thoughts must have been running on, continually turning to the moment when he had to determine his own destiny – this man with a wife and children, a mother and father and friends in his far distant homeland.

Langsdorff looked a shadow of himself, men reported, seeing him walking the still and silent ship, a man who was sealing his own fate in the death of the *Graf Spee*.

The battleship made her last voyage while demolition charges were still being positioned. She began to move again, turning until she came out of the channel and her nose ran into soft mud. There was to be talk about this in British and Allied newspapers later – that the dirty Hun had deliberately sunk his ship in the fairway of a nation which had given him sanctuary. But there was nothing mean or vindictive about Langsdorff; the evidence is that he quietly took his ship to a place where it would not endanger or embarrass other shipping and there destroyed her.

He ordered the anchor to be let go when she was finally aground, and again this was probably to ensure that the *Graf Spee* would not drift from the grave he had chosen for her and settle inside the deep water channel. Then the *Tacoma* sent launches across to the bigger ship and took off her scuttling party, Langsdorff last of all – a captain who turned before stepping from his ship and saluted a flag he could by now have hated, the mighty swastika that had filled with dread the hearts of so many British seamen in the past months.

The *Tacoma* and attendant ships drew to a safe distance, and then in sombre silence every man aboard them stood and watched the deserted, motionless ship, silhouetted against the dying sun. At 2054 the end came. Deliberately, Langsdorff timed to coincide the destruction of the *Graf Spee* with the exact moment of the setting of the sun.

Suddenly, startling even though they had been waiting for it, a mighty explosion flamed inside the ship; the decks seemed to erupt upwards, debris flying high into the air as the sullen roar smote the ears of the watching crew. Immediately a tremendous fire began to rage from stem to stern of her, and the evening sky became black with a towering, spreading column of smoke.

On board the *Tacoma* and the Argentine barge, at the moment of the explosion, every man came to attention and gave the Nazi salute ... every man except Langsdorff, faithful

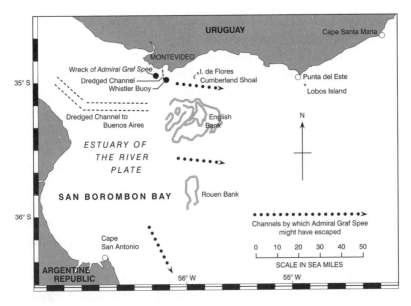

Above: Map of the estuary of the River Plate showing possible exit channels available to the German heavy cruiser *Admiral Graf Spee* after the battle, along with the position of the wreck.

to the old tradition in this hour of agony for him. Langsdorff's salute was the old one, the one that had been used between honourable men long before the upstart Hitler.

Ashore, a tremendous gasp went up from the spectators as they witnessed the destruction of the *Graf Spee*. The people around the harbour were near enough to feel the concussion of the successive explosions aboard the *Graf Spee* as her magazines became ignited. The night sky became white with the flashes of the exploding ammunition. Every moment of it was described and broadcast by the throngs of radio commentators. Afterwards the various agencies cabled their stories to their newspapers.

The United Press reported: "The *Graf Spee* sank, blazing after an explosion which is believed to have occurred in the magazine, off Montevideo tonight, and only the top of her superstructure is now showing.

"It is believed that none of the crew were killed in this spectacular scuttling of the great pocket battleship, which was the pride of the German Navy. The fire, which broke out after the explosion, spread from stem to stern, and smoke poured into the skies from the burning mass." A later report from the United Press said: "The *Graf Spee* is resting on the bottom of the estuary, just outside the channel leading to the outer harbour of Montevideo. It appears unlikely that she will sink completely out of sight.

"Ships in harbour blew their sirens when the explosion aboard the *Graf Spee* was reported. Crowds rushed to vantage points to see the end of the battleship."

From the harbour of Montevideo streamed a great array of small craft, hastening to the scene of the explosion. Uruguay was making the most of the spectacle. But well ahead of them was a Uruguayan gunboat and tug containing port officials, uncertain how to act in the circumstances.

They seemed particularly annoyed by the sight of the Argentine flag in their waters, and the fact that the crew of the *Graf Spee* were now being shipped towards Buenos Aires. The gunboat stopped the flotilla and would not let it proceed, even though Langsdorff came aboard the tug and explained that everything he had done had been with the assent of the Uruguayan authorities.

It was a curious moment, one demonstrating the lack of personal feeling when men go to war. For aboard the tug were British officers and officials; enemies were shoulder to shoulder, and yet there was no incident, no hostile display towards the German captain. Polite Britishers stood aside and allowed Langsdorff to make his peace with the outraged Uruguayans.

Radio messages were exchanged with the shore and finally, apparently reluctantly, Langsdorff and his men were allowed to proceed across the estuary to Buenos Aires. Behind them the ship they had deserted seemed to writhe in agony as the fire burnt out her heart and she began to settle.

The British cruisers were too far away to interfere with the scuttling plans, and only came up in the last light of day as the ship lay burning furiously. When they realised that their enemy had been destroyed, everyone aboard the British ships went crazy, cheering with delirious delight. Now beyond any dispute the Battle of the River Plate had ended in victory for them.

During the early night *Achilles* and *Ajax* came together near to the inferno that marked the *Graf Spee*. The crews cheered each other until they could hardly make a sound for hoarseness. It was one of the greatest moments of their lives, perhaps with only one greater moment to come ... when they returned to receive the homage of their respective countries.

In all parts of the world the news was received, and in many parts it was twisted to suit home consumption. In Germany the story was played down at first. In fact only eleven lines were given to the scuttling, and this was sandwiched between other war news items. The German population must have been bewildered at the change in manner – one moment the story filling the headlines, and the next dismissed as trivial and hardly worth mention.

A communique was issued on December 18 by the German High Command which stated, "Between the Moselle and the Palatinate Forest there was somewhat livelier artillery fire on both sides.

"The German Air Force reconnoitred over Eastern France and the North Sea. German aeroplanes reached the Shetland Isles and Portsmouth in the South. In several places German planes chased British patrol coastal boats, and one patrol boat was bombed and sunk. In the evening British planes attempted to reach the German coast.

"The *Graf Spee* was not granted the time which was necessary to make the ship seaworthy by the Uruguayan Government. The Leader and Supreme Commander gave orders to the Commander to destroy the warship outside Uruguayan waters."

Afterwards further communiqués were issued which enlarged upon the theme and somehow managed to make a triumph of the scuttling of their prize battleship. To distract home attention, the story of insults to the dead of the *Graf Spee* was also revived. The German News Agency repeated the charge on December 20: "It has just become known that during the funeral of the thirty-six fallen sailors of the *Admiral Graf Spee* outrageous scenes took place. British seamen from several ships lying in the harbour spat on the coffins of the procession, caterwauling went on in the background during the funeral sermon for the fallen, and the climax of this behaviour was reached when, immediately after the burial, they threw a dead dog on to the tomb of the German sailors."

It is interesting to speculate about the battle and wonder how the war at sea might have been altered, so far as British fortunes were concerned, if the German ship had gained the victory over its three smaller opponents.

On paper there is no doubt that the British cruisers were completely out-matched by the battleship. If a more resolute, less gentlemanly personality than Captain Langsdorff had commanded the *Graf Spee*, perhaps the British ships might have been smashed out of existence, leaving the Germans triumphant in the battle and with a morale heightened by victory over the dreaded British Navy. Encouraged by the success, it could have emboldened German naval strategy with dire results to British shipping. As it was, defeat induced an inferiority complex which immobilised, or largely immobilised, Hitler's remaining surface fleet.

The victory at the River Plate did more than merely destroy

a pocket battleship, and with it the myth of invincibility, it induced a policy of ultra-caution on the part of Hitler's surface fleet which amounted in cases to a state of immobility. Not the best way of conducting a naval war.

Chapter 24

Langsdorff's Death

The Battle of the River Plate was not yet over, however, certainly not so far as the headlines of the world's newspapers were concerned. On December 20, 1939, less than three days after the destruction of the *Graf Spee*, the newspapermen who still lingered in Buenos Aires had another sensational story.

Captain Langsdorff had shot himself.

Many of his officers and men had guessed the fate he had intended for himself, but even so it shocked them that he should have died, purposelessly unless honour is a matter of count for some men.

The personnel from the German battleship were quartered in the Naval Arsenal in Buenos Aires while discussions as to their future were conducted at very high level by Doctor Langmann. On the evening of the 19th, Captain Langsdorff called a last meeting of his men in the Naval Arsenal and made a farewell speech to them. He did not directly inform them of his contemplated action, but too many unhappily sensed why he addressed them as he did, in terms of a man saying good-bye forever.

When they were dismissed, Langsdorff went the rounds of his fellow officers and distributed mementoes, his few personal possessions to them, and shook hands for the last time.

Then he went to his room, a man alone now in a world in which he no longer wished to remain. A man who must have been thinking of his loved ones who would never see him again, and might never understand what he was about to do. But to Langsdorff, ordered to scuttle his ship and not fight as tradition had bred in him – Langsdorff who knew he would have the sneers and scorn of the mean-hearted if he went on living – life was no longer endurable. Even here in Buenos Aires, reputedly friendly towards Germany, his actions were being violently criticised. He flinched when they shouted "Coward!" at him.

In the loneliness of night, Langsdorff took out the flag he had first served before he had been made to pay respect to the bastard insignia of a politically vicious creed, the Nazism of Germany. Laying the Imperial Flag of the Germany he had been born into on the floor, Langsdorff shot himself.

It was the end of a man bred to war yet exercising the greatest humanity whenever possible, even to the risk of his own and his ship's safety. Perhaps with more Langsdorffs there might be no wars to demand a strain upon the humanity of the participants.

His career was a fine and meritorious record of promotion, yet it brought him to an end which served only to be used by the propagandists of the warring countries.

A gesture of repudiation of the Führer's Nazi policies, shouted the Press of the world unfriendly to Hitler, and blew into headlines the significance of his choice of flag for a funeral shroud. A man hounded to his death on the eve of internment by an unfriendly neutral state, was a version put out in Germany.

Langsdorff's funeral on December 21 was again a much publicised affair. He was given full military honours, and now there was no sign of hostility from the enormous crowds who lined the route to the German cemetery outside Buenos Aires.

Attending were representatives of the Argentine Army and Navy, the German Ambassador to the Argentine, and the officers and men of the *Graf Spee*. Slowly pacing with the funeral cortège was a British representative. He was Captain Pottinger, of the S.S. *Ashlea*, representing the other British captives who had come into Montevideo aboard the German battleship. There was no glad malice in their hearts at the end of the man who had lost them their ships; for they remembered him only as a man who had done his best to lessen for them the discomforts of war. Their appreciation was shown by the wreath which Captain Pottinger carried, bought by a subscription raised among the ex-prisoners.

Another wreath was sent on behalf of the man who had caused the whole tragedy, and not for Langsdorff only. The card bore the name of … Hitler.

The Argentine Government had behaved with the greatest courtesy towards the German sailors, and had given full honour to the *Graf Spee* captain in his death. Nevertheless, they were a neutral state, and their neutrality called for action so far as the remaining Germans were concerned. An announcement was made that they were to be interned.

Instantly another diplomatic battle raged over the fate of the *Graf Spee*'s crew. Berlin screamed that it was outrageous discrimination and no act of neutrality. The officers and crew of the *Graf Spee* were equivalent of shipwrecked mariners and should be repatriated, they said.

Britain stood by ready to talk strongly if Argentine showed signs of weakening before Nazi bluster and intimidation, but in the end the Argentine Government announced that their decision was final – the Germans would go into captivity for the duration of war in accordance with the Rules on International Warfare.

At first the Germans were put on parole and allowed their freedom, but some disturbances between them and pro-British sections of the Argentine public in the end compelled more forcible internment.

Pressure was also brought to bear upon the Uruguayan Government, because of the wounded who still lay in hospital there. But the Uruguayans also were not to be intimidated, and the forty men in hospital were duly interned.

A minor victory for the Germans, a dozen officers and men were permitted to join the German Legation staff in Montevideo. It was a small consolation for the loss of 1,140 young Germans, killed or interned as a result of that remarkable interception of their ship by the then Commodore Harwood at dawn that day off the River Plate.

The action was a tremendous fillip to British prestige in the Americas, and brought many tributes to the gallant men who had fought the battle for Britain. One was a cheque for £1,000, subscribed by the British community in Argentine whose interests had been defended, for distribution among the dependants of those killed in the battle.

Both Argentine and Uruguay were permitted to pay tribute to the victors. On a memorable day after the German crew had been interned (along with the crew of the *Tacoma*, for by its actions in refuelling a belligerent warship it had become subject to the rules of warfare, too), the *Ajax* came slowly into the inner harbour at Montevideo.

She had to pass close to where the blackened, still smouldering hull of the *Graf Spee* (soon to be sold for £1,000 to a scrap iron firm of salvagers), lay sunk in shallow waters. An enormous crowd lined the harbour and gave a mighty welcome to Sir Henry Harwood and his men. When the crew came ashore they found the city was theirs, the generous-hearted Uruguayans giving them the time of their lives.

In Argentine, too, it was much the same. The New Zealand ship, *Achilles*, received a victor's welcome as she came into Buenos Aires, where she was permitted to stay for forty-eight hours in order to refuel and revictual.

Later, much later, the *Exeter* was to receive her ovation, too.

Chapter 25

The Victors Return Home

After the battle, my Lords of the Admiralty were disposed to be gracious towards the cruisers of Harwood's squadron. When repairs permitted the voyage, each would return to its own country, *Ajax* and *Exeter* to England, and *Achilles* to New Zealand. It was felt that the crews were deserving of home leave, in any event.

So, before dawn on January 21, 1940, *Ajax* crept quietly into Plymouth Sound, her mainmast still missing. Word went swiftly round the town, and large crowds assembled to cheer her all the way to Devonport Dockyard. When she arrived there, she was greeted by the Commander-in-Chief of the Western Approaches, Admiral Sir Martin Dunbar-Nasmith, V.C., and the Deputy Lord Mayor of Plymouth, Alderman Modley. It was a fine reception, and the people of Plymouth gave the crew of the *Ajax* a most heart-warming welcome when they came ashore.

The big regret was that Rear-Admiral Sir Henry Harwood was not with *Ajax*. However, he had transferred his flag to another cruiser, and had remained in command of the South America station.

Glad though the people of Plymouth were to receive the cruiser, however, the fact was that *Ajax* was a Chatham ship, and their heart and interest was with *Exeter*, manned by West

Country men. No disrespect to *Ajax*, of course, but it was their own sons and husbands they wanted to see.

Exeter was a long time in returning to England. In Devon they knew she was badly shattered and only with difficulty was able to make herself seaworthy in the faraway Falkland Islands. Perhaps she would never make the journey through the thousands of miles of hostile seas, crippled as she was, they began to think ...

One morning in February, 1940, as light slowly brightened to reveal the war-time shipping crowding the harbour of Plymouth, there was a gasp as someone recognised a familiar vessel.

Like lightning the cry went round the city – "*Exeter*'s back!" *Exeter*, their own ship, the cruiser that had taken the enemy's fire and lost so terribly so that victory might be obtained, she was lying at anchor about a mile from the Hoe.

All over Plymouth people began to race to see her come into Devonport. From houses and shops and offices, people streamed in their gladness, until the Hoe and all vantage points overlooking the harbour were black with people straining to see the battered ship of which they were so proud. Slowly the *Exeter* began to move up channel towards her berth, coming closer all the while, so that they could see her crew lined up on the decks and see – but not hear – the ship's band of the Royal Marines as they played the *Exeter*'s own song, "We are the *Exeter*, straight from the West."

It was a moment of tremendous emotion for everyone concerned. The crew would never forget it. For them everything seemed worthwhile – that terrible thrashing they had received, the days of uncertainty and discomfort while they limped to the Falkland Isles. And that hazardous voyage home from Port Stanley.

No announcement had been made to the British public of

Exeter's return, but it seemed as though Berlin had known she was on her way. The crew would never forget that voyage, either. Word went round the ship that Hitler had ordered his submarine commanders to sink the *Exeter* at all costs, to give him a propaganda triumph as a postscript to the battle he had lost.

At all stages of their voyage home they were under escort – but then the *Exeter* was still damaged and unable to fight effectively and needed to be protected. Day after day there were warnings of submarines, and their escorts went racing away to drop depth charges. It became monotonous. Even a few hours before entering Plymouth Sound, there was a daring attempt made to get *Exeter*, and among the men it was said that a record number of submarines had been destroyed on that voyage – some put the score as high as fourteen. It was a heavy price to pay to achieve a propaganda point, and in the end it achieved nothing.

Exeter was there, safe if not sound, in Plymouth Bay, and she was coming in to the reception of her life. The enormous crowd cheered her until it seemed impossible for human beings to make such a sound. It was joyful, deliriously happy. And every workman along the harbour had picked up a hammer or lump of metal and was adding to the din by banging away at iron plating as if their lives depended on it.

The *Exeter* was back. No one would ever forget that day.

As she passed Mount Wise, headquarters of the Commander-in-Chief, the First Lord of the Admiralty was there to take the salute, Mr. Winston Churchill. With him to do honour to the gallant *Exeter* was a very distinguished gathering – the Chancellor of the Exchequer, Sir John Simon, First Sea Lord Sir Dudley Pound, and Sir Martin Dunbar-Nasmith, V.C. And others – many other distinguished men and women were there to pay tribute to the returning heroes.

When the *Exeter* had passed Mount Wise, Mr. Churchill and other distinguished guests boarded a motor launch and followed the ship the three miles to her berth alongside the dockyard wall, to the accompaniment of nonstop cheering all the way.

The party boarded the *Exeter*, all hands were mustered on the quarter-deck, and Mr. Churchill gave the following address:-

"In this sombre dark winter, when, apart from the Navy, we have been at war and yet not at war; in these long winter months, when we have had to watch the agony of Poland and now of Finland, the brilliant action of the Plate, in which you played a memorable part, came like a flash of light and colour on the scene, carrying with it an encouragement to all who are fighting – to ourselves and to our Allies; and carrying with it the cause of rejoicing to free men and to free people all over the world. You cannot but recognize that you had the fortune to be on the spot when the opportunity came. All over the world, as you know, your comrades in the Royal Navy are ardently and eagerly awaiting for an opportunity to emulate your example. Here at Plymouth, where our flotillas guard the western approaches and where, under Admiral Nasmith's direction, such notable successes have been attained in the war against the U-boats, here we are specially able to congratulate you upon the fortune which enabled you to fight an action in the old style, instead of a long and intricate struggle with the mines and the U-boats which our comrades in the flotillas have been waging here.

"This great action will long be told in song and story. When you came up the river this morning, when you entered the harbour and saw the crowds cheering on the banks, one may almost think that there were other spectators in the great shades of the past, carrying us back to the days of Drake and Raleigh, to the great sea dogs of the olden times. If their spirits brooded on this scene you would be able to say to them, 'We, your descendants, still make war and have not forgotten the lessons you taught.'

"Many months, perhaps some years, of anxious struggle lies before us, and we face the future in a spirit of serious resolve. You have all lost good comrades and shipmates who are not here with us today, but you are here, and your gallant ship is back to cheer the hearts of your fellow-countrymen; and you have come back with the firm knowledge of having worked notably, and faithfully accomplished in a worthy cause, with your honours gathered and with your duty done."

After the speech-making, the men received the glad news that they could go ashore. First to go, it was noticed, was the ship's cat which had survived the battle along with the ship's canary. She went down the gangplank ahead of the shore party, and in her way perhaps she celebrated the return, just as the eager men were intent on celebrating it with their friends and families.

But the celebrations certainly did not end on February 15 for the crews of the *Ajax* and *Exeter*. Next day three hundred officers and men of both ships paraded at Stonehouse Bridge and then marched to the Guildhall, feted as heroes the whole of the way. There was a civic luncheon for them, followed by more speeches.

In distant Auckland, on February 22, the scenes were repeated, New Zealand fashion, as their proud ship, the *Achilles*, returned to her home port at Auckland. At the Heads a great fleet of small craft was there to greet her, and in the harbour every whistle and siren blew a tumultuous welcome to her gallant crew. To pay their tribute to their fighting men came Lord Galwey, Governor-General of New Zealand, the deputy Prime Minister, the Hon. Peter Fraser, and other members of the Cabinet.

Auckland was decorated and beflagged, and a great procession was formed to march with the heroes to the Auckland Town Hall where they were addressed by Mr.

Fraser. It was expected, he said, that the men would live up to the highest traditions of the Royal Navy, but they had exceeded anything that could have been expected by friend or foe. At the end of his speech telegrams were read from the Governments of Britain and Australia and the French Minister of Marine. Maori representatives presented Captain Parry with a beautiful mat of native design.

Mr. Eden, Secretary of State for Dominion Affairs, on behalf of the United Kingdom Government, sent the following message to the New Zealand Government on the occasion of the *Achilles'* return to Auckland:

"His Majesty's Government in the United Kingdom have learnt with great pleasure of the arrival in New Zealand of H.M.S. *Achilles* fresh from the great battle which led to the destruction of the *Admiral Graf Spee*. The heroic and skilful part which she played in that notable victory will long be remembered in the annals of naval history and has added lustre to the record of New Zealand's achievements in the struggle for liberty and justice in which we are engaged. New Zealand may well be proud of her sons who have given such signal proof of the contribution which New Zealand is making towards the common victory.

"We feel it particularly appropriate that H.M.S. *Achilles* should arrive home in New Zealand on the day on which the officers and men of H.M.S. *Ajax* and H.M.S. *Exeter* are being reviewed by His Majesty the King. We should have been happy if it had been possible for the officers and men of H.M.S. *Achilles* to be similarly honoured in London at the same time, and although circumstances have not rendered this feasible we can assure them that the gallant part which they took in the action will be present in the minds of all here.

"To all the officers and men of H.M.S. *Achilles* His Majesty's Government in the United Kingdom send warmest greetings and best wishes for their future welfare and success."

Even that was not the end to the tributes paid to the victors of the River Plate Battle. With the return of two of the three cruisers to Britain, there came a demand that a national as well as local tribute should be paid to the men of these ships. Tumultuous though their reception had been in Plymouth, it was felt that London should also be permitted to pay tribute on behalf of the nation for whom the battle had been fought.

So, on February 23, 760 officers and men of the two cruisers were brought by special train to Waterloo Station, London, from which they marched over Westminster Bridge to the Horse Guards Parade, headed by the Royal Marine Band from Chatham.

London turned out for the occasion, solidly flanking the route, and giving the finely marching men a truly tremendous ovation – probably a million people were there to see them and pay homage to their gallantry. Marching with the men were six Merchant Navy captains who had been prisoners on board the *Graf Spee*.

In a reserved corner of the Horse Guards Parade was a group of relatives of men who had lost their lives fighting for their country.

When the ships' companies had been drawn up into the three sides of a hollow square, a door opened in the nearby Admiralty, and out came His Majesty, King George VI, wearing the uniform of an Admiral-of-the-Fleet. Behind were the Duke of Kent, Mr. Winston Churchill and the whole Board of Admiralty, the Prime Minister, Mr. Neville Chamberlain, Cabinet Ministers and other notabilities.

From a balcony overlooking the Parade, Her Majesty Queen Elizabeth with other distinguished ladies watched the colourful ceremony below. Rarely can any parade have had such a notable audience.

The ships' captains were presented to His Majesty, who then inspected the parade and afterwards awarded battle honours. Afterwards came another triumphal march through London's cheering streets to the historic Guildhall, where they were addressed by the Lord Mayor of London, and then by Mr. Churchill. There were more speeches, more telegrams, messages from the wounded in the Falkland Islands and Montevideo. A wonderful day for the men, who enjoyed it but were ready to protest that too much was being made of them.

It was the end-piece to the Battle of the River Plate. Within weeks the men would be back on duty, for the war was beginning to take a grim and ominous turn and the time for junketing and celebrations was past.

They served their country well in the years to follow, those men of *Exeter*, *Ajax* and *Achilles*. More were to give their lives, some in battle, some as prisoners of the Japanese when the *Exeter* was sunk in action in the Pacific later in the war. Many more were to be wounded, sometimes crippled for life.

Chapter 26

The 'Altmark Incident'

But the end of the *Graf Spee* incident did not come with the scuttling of the battered pocket battleship. Two hundred and ninety-nine victims of the marauder were still in German hands and that was an intolerable position for the British public to accept.

From the moment it was known that British seamen were imprisoned aboard the supply ship, *Altmark*, the demand went up – "Get that ship!"

Mr. Churchill gave the order to find the *Altmark* and rescue the seamen at all costs, and so began another gigantic hunt across the world's seas for a solitary vessel … a ship which seemed to have disappeared with the sinking of the *Graf Spee*. Weeks went by, and in that time there was not the slightest trace reported of the prison ship, though every ship in the world was on the look-out for her. Then, on February 2, 1940, an enemy report was issued that the *Altmark* had reached the safety of a German port. German elation was tremendous at the outwitting of the mighty British sea power, and a corresponding depression settled over islands not unused to depressions.

But there was a slight error in the German report. It was inaccurate in an important aspect; for the *Altmark* on February 2 was several thousand miles away from Germany. The report was a bluff, designed to make the British call off their hunt and so permit the German ship to slip through the North Sea undetected; but it did not deceive the Admiralty who continued their relentless search for the vessel.

On December 7 the *Altmark* had parted from the pocket battleship. A few days later her commander, Captain Dau, received a signal that the *Graf Spee* had been severely damaged in battle with British cruisers and had had to seek the shelter of a South American port. Later came a further signal informing him of the end of the raider, though this news was kept from the prisoners.

This meant that the supply ship had no ship to supply – her purpose in southern waters had come to an end. In any event, the *Altmark* had been long at sea and required a refit, as well as leave for her crew, all of which indicated a long and hazardous trip back to Germany.

At the same time, Berlin woke up to the propaganda value of the prisoners aboard *Altmark*. The loss of the *Graf Spee* had been a tremendous blow to the prestige of the German navy, and it was felt that to parade captured British seamen in Germany, would help to restore some of the shattered morale. Orders were therefore sent to Captain Dau to sail for Germany; he was told to take every precaution so as to get his ship through without detection, and at once preparations were made to hold triumphal processions through Berlin, Hamburg, Bremen and other principal cities. The parade of prisoners would be something like a Roman triumph, more valuable to the morale of the German people than any amount of face-saving propaganda over the *Graf Spee* disaster.

But first the *Altmark* had to sail a distance of something like fifteen thousand miles, through waters almost entirely hostile to German shipping. For the Royal Navy was certainly in command of the seas late in 1939 and early 1940. Captain Dau turned south, heading away from Germany, until he was in the cold waters of the South Atlantic. Here he loitered for three weeks in order to give the hunt a chance to die down. It was an uncomfortable period for crew and prisoners alike, for the days were stormy, and the cold was penetrating.

For the prisoners, with little spare clothing to wrap round them, it proved to be a grim and anxious time. Accommodation was bad. They were herded into comfortless holds, without sanitary conveniences or electric light, rarely allowed on deck and with little to pass away the hours of boredom. Their thoughts could not have been very sustaining, either – their fate seemed to be a choice between eventual imprisonment in Germany or drowning following action at sea.

The captain of the *Huntsman*, incidentally, was with the prisoners, though he could have been with the other merchant ships' captains in the *Graf Spee*. But he had had Lascars aboard his ship and was not sure they would be well treated in the *Altmark*, so he had applied to Captain Langsdorff to be transferred to the prison ship to look after them. This was granted.

Conditions were bad aboard the *Altmark*, and the Press of the world friendly to Britain dubbed it a hell-ship and called Captain Dau a brutal fiend. Yet some of the men who were captive did not altogether agree with this. They pointed out that conditions were dictated to Dau and he could do little to improve them. He had to accommodate this large number of men and the only space available for the purpose was inadequate and quite unsuitable. Again prisoners outnumbered his crew by almost two to one, and this meant strict security arrangements and therefore little time each day for the prisoners to exercise on deck.

In some ways he was considerate. He allowed coir fibre to be placed on the floor of the ammunition lockers to make comfortable beds, and he sent down Persian rugs, booty from one of the sunken prizes, and later some of the prisoners' own bedding and belongings, taken from their ships.

But in other respects he was not considerate. He was quick

with his punishments, clapping offenders into solitary confinement on a diet of bread and water, and restricting opportunities for sick seamen to visit the ship's doctor.

As a personality, Captain Dau appeared in contradictory guises to his prisoners. He was elderly – sixty-seven, according to his own statements to one of the British captive officers. He never appeared in uniform, but always wore a grey or blue suit. He spoke English well, only hesitating occasionally over a word, and was said to have been a prisoner of war in England during the First World War. This experience, so it was said, accounted for his dislike amounting to hatred of the British, though it is unlikely that in England he could have suffered as much in captivity as the British seamen in the *Altmark*.

Dau, who said he had commanded a submarine in the 1914-18 war, was probably a Nazi. Certainly there was much saluting and heiling of Hitler aboard his ship, with pictures of the Führer decorating the *Altmark* in a profusion which annoyed some of the British prisoners.

Early on in the "cruise," Captain Dau called all the prisoners together while he addressed them. His tone was moderate enough to begin with, though uncompromising. "I know it isn't your fault that you are prisoners," he said, "but I have no sympathy for you, all the same. If you do not obey orders, I will use force to make you obey."

Then quickly he seemed to lose control over himself and almost raved at his captive audience. German prisoners in South Africa weren't being treated as well as they, he shouted. In Africa they were being herded into native huts and were forced to sleep on the floor. To his Nazi mind, it was an affront for a German to have to live in a "native's" hut.

"This ship," Captain Dau told them in his angry English, "was on a peaceful mission from Port Arthur to Rotterdam when you English forced a war on us. But England will not win this war, and this time there will be no Treaty of

Versailles. You will have to put up with the conditions in this ship because we have no colonies, like South Africa, where we can place our prisoners. But soon Germany will have her colonies again."

He ranted a good deal, not always clear in what he was trying to say, jumping swiftly from one thought to another. But though he antagonised some of his prisoners, so that one British captain afterwards said, "They sought to humiliate us. Conditions were pretty rotten, and treatment was certainly not humane," most did not complain much about their treatment, and seemed without rancour towards Dau, whatever the Press of Great Britain said about the matter.

"Dau never came down and bullied us," said one of the British officers, a tolerant appraisal from a man who certainly was no better treated than his comrades.

When the prisoners learned, as inevitably they learned, that the *Graf Spee* had been defeated in battle with British cruisers, there were some who said it would not have happened if Dau had commanded the pocket battleship instead of the too-gentlemanly Langsdorff. Dau, the disciplinarian, who took no nonsense from anyone, whose courage was demonstrably high, would have fought a bitter fight, and such a man could have turned those big 11-inch guns to victory. Again, that was a compliment indeed, to come from men fretting in his captivity.

The crew of the *Altmark* seemed to be pretty decent fellows, on the whole seeming sorry to see the misfortune of their comrades of the sea. In many ways they tried to ease their lot, smuggling tobacco and papers down to them, and occasionally extra food.

Not so the guard which had come over from the *Graf Spee* to watch over them. Twenty young German sailors, under a youthful lieutenant named Schmidt, were supposed to be guarding the prisoners. They proved to be unpleasant young bounders, disliked as much by the British captives as by the

Altmark's crew. As the weary weeks went by, the German seamen and sailors became involved in quarrels and even fights, until Dau forced them to keep to their separate quarters except when on duty.

Schmidt seemed rather an amiable man, though he apparently considered it part of his duty to reduce the morale of the British seamen as much as possible. Time after time he came up with rumours which should have been disturbing. One day he told Captain Brown, "Captain, the war is going badly for you. Now we have sunk the *Barham*."

Brown took his pipe from his mouth. "Do you," he asked coldly, "know any other funny stories?" The Merchant Navy took some getting down.

A curious thing happened soon after the *Altmark* abruptly sailed for the colder, southern seas. The prisoners' food became better. There was more of it, and the rations contained unusual luxuries. Once they even had crystallised cherries.

The solution to the mystery came when the ship's carpenter, a friendly, gossippy German who had lived for twenty years in America, one day whispered to the prisoners, "The *Graf Spee* ... *kaput!*"

"*Kaput?* Sunk?" Incredulously the prisoners crowded round the little German. He seemed uneasy at their interest and backed away, his eyes watching apprehensively to see if any *Altmark* officers were watching.

Within minutes all the prisoners in the various holds knew the gossip. The *Graf Spee* had been sunk! The British Navy was not lying in corners, doing nothing. The White Ensign was out and triumphant again, and that brought hope to them. The Navy would get the *Altmark* just as it had got the *Graf Spee*. Then they would be free, and that thought was as intoxicating as alcohol to the prisoners.

But the news caused trouble for someone aboard the *Altmark* – the ship's carpenter. Some unthinking British seaman had to collar Lieutenant Schmidt when he came the rounds of the prison holds and demand, "Hey, what's this talk about the *Graf Spee* being *kaput*?"

Schmidt looked at him, astonished. Then he came forward quickly, demanding excitedly, "How did you know that? Who told you? You are not supposed to know such +things."

He rushed off to report to Captain Dau and there was an appalling fuss that went on for hours. Suspicion finally concentrated on the unhappy little carpenter, who confessed and was slung into solitary. The prisoners – especially the man who had opened his mouth too widely – were horrified when they heard that Captain Dau was going to execute the carpenter. Dau was really in a savage mood, and they felt he was quite capable of killing the little German. Then, in some mysterious way, they heard that the ship's doctor had intervened most strongly and got the poor wretch fifteen days on bread and water instead of a firing squad or a rope at the end of a yardarm.

This doctor was a most popular man with the prisoners.

He was strong enough to stand up to Dau, and he treated the prisoners on equal terms with the Germans. From the beginning he made no bones about it that he didn't think Hitler was going to win the war, and would often talk to the prisoners about it. "When is it going to end?" he asked gloomily one day. "It's only beginning, doc," the British seamen promised grimly.

"It would end more quickly if you got rid of Churchill," the German doctor said.

In which he was probably right.

The British seamen, closely guarded and mostly confined to their dreary holds, kept in touch with the life of the *Altmark* as much as anything through the Lascars from the *Huntsman*. These men were allowed the run of the ship, being treated as unintelligent, harmless creatures rather than men, despised and not to be considered as possible makers of trouble. They had to work in the ship's galleys, and do other work about the *Altmark*.

The Lascars, incidentally, had the roughest time aboard the ship. They had the poorest quarters, and came last in the matter of rations, and in other respects.

As an example, ten bowls of water were put out each morning (unless the prisoners were being punished for some infringement of rules) for the ablutions of close on three hundred men. Mates and chief engineers had first go at the water, to be followed by the white seamen. Then, and then only, the Lascars were permitted to wash. Yet their captain afterwards said they were the cleanest men aboard ship.

The German carpenter was at length released and was welcomed by the prisoners. For days he would not talk to them, but at length, an inveterate and uncontrollable gossip, he had to tell them more news. This time it was bad.

"The *Ark Royal* has been bombed and sunk, and Russia has declared war on England."

It was disturbing. The carpenter had been right about the *Graf Spee*, and perhaps he was right with his other information, they thought uneasily. But this time they refused to believe him. If they started to believe such things, their morale would rot in their unpleasant confinement, and they did not want to give in because giving in would have made imprisonment even more unpleasant. Hope kept them going through those dragging days in the wild, cold seas of the far South Atlantic.

They were bad days. One quart of brackish water a day, poor food, and at the most an hour and three-quarters out of twenty-four exercising on deck – until even this was stopped.

Several times deck exercise was cancelled, so that for ten days on end the prisoners had to remain below, wet from the dripping of condensation on the roof and walls of their prison. Once it happened because a prisoner threw a bottle containing an S.O.S. message into the sea while at exercise.

Instantly a lookout raised the alarm, the *Altmark* slowed, came round in a circle, and the bottle was fished out with the aid of a long-handled net. Another time trouble came their way as a result of a careless action on the part of a model maker. Sailorlike, many of the men spent their enforced leisure whittling beautiful models out of wood. Even during deck exercise periods, they would continue their work, and one day one of the men unthinkingly threw his wooden chippings overboard. The action was misconstrued and there was trouble for the unhappy man and confinement for his comrades.

The friendly *Altmark* seamen sometimes held whispered conversations with the prisoners. The British seamen were astonished at the opinions held by their German comrades.

The crew of the *Altmark* were of the opinion that the British people were the cruellest race on earth, not fit to call themselves civilised. They sincerely believed that in England the practice still persisted of cutting off a man's hand if he were found guilty of theft. When every British seaman present promptly lifted two hands and boasted they were all a lot of bloody thieves, the Germans looked puzzled but unshaken in their beliefs.

The English were a brutal people, who would have to pay for their brutality. They only hoped they would never become prisoners in the hands of the Englishers. Yet they were decent in their behaviour, for all the stuff that had been pumped into them.

Another opinion, quite honestly held, was that the war was going very badly for the English. "We are winning the war," they would strut, "and by now you have very few ships left in your navy".

"And the *Graf Spee* to you!" was the usual British retort to this astonishing opinion.

Christmas came. It should have been a melancholy time for the prisoners, but they rose to the occasion and somehow made a party of it. Captain Brown, who had brought some stores aboard with him, shared out thirty pounds of tobacco in two-ounce tins.

New Year also was celebrated with a great deal of noise and singing, winding up with "Auld Lang Syne". It was a brave effort at keeping up morale, for they had little to sing about, in the driving, icy winds of the near-Antarctic sea, prisoners in the hands of a dangerous enemy. But they sang, as much to keep up their own spirits as to show the enemy they weren't getting downhearted. The Navy would come and haul them out, they would say confidently, within the hearing of the Germans, and they believed in it implicitly themselves.

By now they were beginning to experiment with cellophane and dried tea leaves. There was a shortage of cigarettes, and the desperation of smokers was such that an offer of a suit of clothes was made for fifty cigarettes.

Tempers were short on all sides during those weeks of aimless cruising in the South Atlantic. The place stank from the oil drums which had to operate as improvised lavatories; some of the men fell ill and the doctor ran out of medicine for them.

One day some of the meat served was bad, and a seaman promptly threw it at the *Graf Spee* guards. He went into solitary before he had time to reflect on his action. Captain Dau would suffer no acts of indiscipline on board. A few days later two men had to be isolated. They had become so depressed and low in condition that the ship's doctor thought they might go mad. It was not a happy time for the men.

More depressing rumours were circulated among the prisoners, but sometimes they misfired. On January 6, Lieutenant Schmidt himself came to tell them important news. They waited for it to come out. They knew they were going to receive a bombshell because of the grim way Schmidt spoke to them. He took his time, but finally the awful truth came out.

Mr. Hore-Belisha had resigned or been dismissed.

Schmidt seemed surprised when the men merely asked, "So what?" If the news had been intended as having a depressing effect, it failed in its purpose.

But later there was other news which made the men uneasy. There was some talk about a peace pact in Rome. Nobody quite understood what it amounted to, but the Germans seemed pleased with themselves, so clearly this pact was not in the best of British interests, whatever it was.

On December 23 a new rumour spread like wildfire round the ship. The pact, the Germans told them, was an agreement which brought Russia *and* Italy into the war against Britain. Now the news began to have a worrying effect on some, though most of the men could still shrug their shoulders and say, "Come off it! Who told you that nonsense?"

The way the rumours circulated made some of the men feel it was part of a deliberate policy by Captain Dau to reduce their morale.

Chapter 27

The Altmark is Found

When it seemed as though they would never leave the grey storm-swept wastes of the south, without warning, the ship changed course and began to steam purposefully north again. It was hours before the prisoners noticed it, and days before they could believe that at last Captain Dau had begun the long and dangerous voyage back to his homeland. All they knew was that the *Altmark* was going at a great lick, so that it was exhilarating in the few minutes they were allowed up on deck, and gradually they were running clear of the cold seas and life was slightly more tolerable in consequence.

They had no illusions about the journey, however. The British Navy would be out hunting for the *Altmark*, and Dau didn't seem to be a quitter. They stood a chance of being rescued, but it was on the cards that many of them would get hurt in the process. Philosophically they stopped worrying about such possibilities and thought of other things.

Merely out of curiosity, they felt impelled to discover what name the *Altmark* was now using. They knew she had changed her identity, and attempted alterations in an effort at disguise, once or twice on the way south, in case they were inadvertently sighted by some other craft. Each time they had learned quite easily of the change of name. A group of prisoners would congregate near the stern. One of their number would be held by his heels and lowered over the stern under cover of his comrades, and in this manner was able to read the name painted thereon.

Once she had been called the *Hangshund*, but now she had an American name, the *Chirqueue*. The knowledge satisfied them, though it appeared to have no practical value. However, putting a sly one over the enemy always boosted their spirits and gave them something to talk and speculate about.

Once the voyage north had started, the officer-prisoners aboard the *Altmark* started to plot her course. To this end, they had made a rough sextant, and were probably close enough most of the time in their calculations.

At the beginning of her voyage, the German ship kept well out into the middle of the Atlantic, retiring at great speed (the *Altmark* was reputed to be able to do twenty-six knots) whenever she saw smoke on the horizon. The men found themselves grudgingly admiring Captain Dau for his fine seamanship during this part of the voyage. In any event, a man had to be good to keep a lightly armed merchant ship at sea all those months without detection with the might of the British Navy out on the hunt for German ships. They only hoped that his luck would run out pretty soon now.

During the passage through tropical waters, the prisoners suffered agonies. They had little water to sustain them, ventilation was appallingly bad in the holds, and save for a few minutes a day they had to exist virtually below decks. This went on for weeks, and severely affected the health of many of them.

But in time the weather grew cooler again, as Captain Dau skilfully brought the *Altmark* almost to the coast of Iceland without detection, and then altered course eastward towards the Norwegian coast, Norway then being a neutral state.

On February 14, 1940, the *Altmark* safely sailed into neutral waters. Now, if she hugged the coast of Norway, she could sail in neutral waters right into Germany. The prisoners knew it, and it was a chilling thought. After nearly five months' captivity for some of them, it now seemed certain they would end up in a German prison camp for the rest of the war. Spirits were low in the *Altmark* prison holds. In Germany they were high. Remarkable preparations were made to receive the *Altmark* – Captain Dau would be honoured for a fine feat of seamanship, and the idea of parading the captive British seamen before the *Herrenvolk* was extended to other cities.

But the British Government hadn't given up the hunt, even though for weeks some of the newspapers had been scathing about the inability of the Navy to find the prison ship.

As the weeks went by, search for the *Altmark* was concentrated on the coast of Norway, it being quite correctly guessed that the prison ship must come down the safe corridor of Norwegian territorial waters to reach Germany. Reconnaissance aircraft of the R.A.F. made a constant patrol of the Norwegian coast, with crews specially briefed to identify the ship.

On February 16, three aircraft took off from England on the routine patrol. Visibility was poor at first, but then later came glorious sunshine to aid the searchers. As they systematically combed the fiord-indented coast for sight of the ship, all the time keeping beyond the three-mile limit so as not to infringe territorial rights, they could see the frozen sea below. Some clear tracks through the pack ice indicated the passage of ships and these were followed wherever practicable.

After a while one of the aircraft saw smoke below and went closer to investigate. The pilot's heart jumped. He had been briefed to look for a tanker-type vessel of 20,000 tons, last seen painted black with yellow or white upperworks. Closer the plane came in towards the ship ploughing a track through the iced-over sea. Then the pilot swore and pulled away. This was like the *Altmark* – black hull and cream upperworks – but her lines were different.

Almost immediately afterwards, the pilot saw another ship below, but this was grey painted. He came in again to investigate … saw a funnel aft, a distinctive feature of the *Altmark*, and at once his hopes shot up again.

He circled at a distance, the other aircraft joining him, and watched the ship below, carefully scrutinising her for further confirmatory features. All three pilots were now excited, pretty sure this was the elusive *Altmark* at last, the first sight of her since the merchant navy captains had reported her existence in Montevideo on December 14, 1939.

But the pilots had to be certain. They all dived on the ship at the same moment, flying towards her stern almost at water level, eyes staring to where the ship's name would reveal itself.

They saw it, but couldn't believe what they saw, so sure had they been that the ship would be using a false name. But there it was in big letters, readable even in the brief moment they flashed across the ship – ALTMARK.

Afterwards the pilots said they all yelled aloud with joy, and their crews were cheering and holding up their thumbs in triumph. The planes pulled up and away, circling a while longer while a dramatic signal was flashed to London: "The *Altmark* is found." There was no sign of life aboard; just an apparently crewless ship steadily forging her way through the pack ice. The pilots had been warned that the ship carried anti-aircraft guns, and they had taken risks in flying in so close, but no attempt was made to gun them, perhaps out of respect for the territorial waters which gave them sanctuary.

The aircraft returned to their base, but by this time the hunt was on. From the Admiralty came orders to British warships to intercept the prison ship; at the same time the news of the discovery of the *Altmark* was broadcast by the B.B.C. and appeared in the evening editions of Britain's war-time newspapers. A whole nation waited anxiously upon the next hours.

They were bitterly disappointing, but even more so for the unfortunate seamen aboard the prison-ship. When they knew they were in Norwegian territorial waters, with all that that implied, they began to feel desperate. They knew that if rescue were to come, it had to come swiftly. Now they were within a few days' sailing of Germany, with the odds against a rescue because to attempt one meant that the British Navy would have to come into conflict with the neutral status of Norway. The gloom and depression in the holds became, in the words of one man, suicidal.

But then hope sprang anew – a Norwegian torpedo boat, *Trygg*, sighted the *Altmark* and must have identified her. This was before the R.A.F. plane found them. She came closer, and the commander of the *Trygg* demanded to be allowed to inspect the ship.

Below they heard voices and sensed the presence of the Norwegian ship alongside them. At once pandemonium broke out as the prisoners tried to indicate their presence to the Norwegians. Men started to beat upon metal with any bar of iron they could lay hands on. They smashed crockery and banged empty fruit cans together, shouted and screamed at the top of their voices, and blew SOS signals on their whistles. It was impossible, they were all agreed, for the ship alongside not to hear that tremendous noise from below deck.

The Germans, probably frantic under the ticklish circumstances, switched off the few lights that had been recently permitted, but the darkness did not in any way diminish the volume of sound. So then the *Altmark*'s crew dragged up hoses and poured sea water in a great flood on the shouting prisoners.

They retaliated by trying to storm through the open hatches, and the Germans had to force them back with cudgels and drawn revolvers. And still the frightful row continued, as the British seamen tried desperately to call attention to their plight.

The Germans then turned on the steam deck-winches in an effort to mask the sound, but even that was ineffectual.

There is no charitable explanation to account for the fact that the Norwegian commander did not appear to notice the appalling noise. Yet after the briefest survey of the ship, noting that the *Altmark* was armed with anti-aircraft guns, the Norwegian torpedo boat went away.

A storm of anger went up, in Norway as well as other countries, when these facts became known, and a defence had to be made of the incident in the Norwegian Parliament on February 19. The defence – that Norway did not know the *Altmark* was carrying prisoners of war through her territorial waters. Considering the fact that the rest of the world knew it, the explanation seemed lame and to the strongly pro-British elements in Norway it was not at all acceptable.

The fact was, of course, that Norway, a little, almost defenceless country, knew that Hitler had his angry eyes on her, and she was only too anxious not to provide an "incident" which could be used as an excuse for aggression by Germany.

Despair gripped the soaked and shivering prisoners when they realised that once again they were alone, and the Norwegians had pulled away. Now it truly seemed the end. If Norway was going to side with Germany, there was nothing to stop the *Altmark* taking them into captivity. They felt the ship moving faster now, as if Dau was anxious to be rid of his responsibility.

Captain Dau was also anxious to punish the men who had tried to defy him when the Norwegian commander was aboard, and he caused a notice to be posted, headed, *Notice to Prisoners*. It read: *On account of today's behaviour of the prisoners, they will get bread and water only tomorrow, instead of the regular meals. Further, I have given an order that neither the Prisoner-Officer, nor the Doctor, will make their rounds after this. Any severe case of sickness can be reported on occasions of handing down the food.*

It was signed, *J.S. Dau, Commander, at sea, Feb.* 15, 1940.

The following day, the prisoners heard aircraft "buzzing" the ship, and hope flamed again as hope will always burn with men of courage and resolution. They had not been forgotten; the R.A.F. had found them.

Chapter 28

The True End to the Last Cruise of Admiral Graf Spee

A British destroyer, racing to the position indicated by the R.A.F. pilots' report, sighted the *Altmark* on the afternoon of February 16. A signal brought up two other destroyers and they ran towards the prison ship, at the same time announcing the news to an Admiralty keyed up for receipt of just such a signal. At once a brief statement was released to the Press, with the hint that the *Altmark* had been sighted. But while a mystified nation waited in unbearable suspense, the hours passed and no report came that the *Altmark* had been boarded and their countrymen released.

The truth was, the situation was proving surprisingly tricky to handle. The prison-ship kept carefully within the three-mile limit of the Norwegian waters, and two Norwegian warships had come out to ensure there was no infringement of her territorial rights. They were the *Skaro* and *Kjell*, also torpedo boats.

Shortly before this dramatic encounter, the *Altmark* had again appeared to run into trouble. The chief naval commander at Bergen was not at all satisfied by the situation and had sent a guard ship to intercept the German vessel. When the guard ship came up, the commander demanded to be allowed to inspect the ship, but this time Captain Dau refused permission. He drew attention to the fact that the *Altmark* flew the Nazi war flag, was armed, and was listed as a German warship. Thus he had every right to refuse inspection, and after some debate the Norwegian guard ship reluctantly drew away.

Then it was found that the *Altmark* was using her radio, and as this was forbidden practice in Norwegian waters by a warship during a time of hostilities, an objection was lodged. Captain Dau said he did not realise he had contravened a Norwegian prohibition and apologised. Anyway, by this time he had reported all he wanted to say to his masters in Berlin.

The *Skaro* and *Kjell* came between the three British destroyers and their quarry and told them to keep their distance. True, the British destroyers could have brushed aside the opposition, but Britain was not at war with Norway, and captains of warships are not encouraged to violate neutral sovereignty.

Captain P.L. Vian, of the destroyer *Cossack*, was commander of the flotilla. Displeased by the situation, yet nevertheless compelled to keep his distance from the big German ship, Vian could only make his report to the Admiralty while keeping pace with the *Altmark* on her dash down the coast towards her homeland.

Time was now running against the British. A tremendous diplomatic battle was being fought in Oslo, the British Minister there putting all pressure possible on the Norwegian Government to detain the *Altmark* and free the prisoners, and the Norwegians finding every technical reason for not taking any action at all. Which meant that the hours were passing and the advantage was transferring from British into German hands.

Late on the day of February 16, it became apparent that the Norwegians, for their own reasons, were not going to budge. Britain had lost the diplomatic battle; Norway would make no attempt to free the imprisoned seamen.

By this time the *Altmark* had turned into Josing Fiord [Jøssingfjord], particularly narrow and difficult to navigate, and there lay to during the last hours of daylight. The two Norwegian warships placed themselves in a position at the mouth of the fiord to prevent any entry by the British destroyers, now ceaselessly patrolling beyond the fiord, much as *Ajax* and *Achilles* had done outside Montevideo.

Aboard the *Cossack*, Captain Vian guessed that the prison-ship was waiting for darkness in order to continue her journey down the coast – either that or she was waiting for German warships or aircraft to come out and rescue her. The surprising thing was that so far no other German craft had come upon the scene, yet it was known that lying at Wilhelmshaven were two powerful new battle cruisers, a heavy, armoured cruiser, and some light cruisers and destroyers. Aboard the *Cossack* they had an uneasy feeling that some of these ships might already be on their way to help the *Altmark*. If that were so, the British would have to act quickly, if they were to act at all; for three small destroyers could not hope to face up to the big German ships.

Impatient, Captain Vian entered territorial waters and approached the entrance to the Josing Fiord. A Norwegian warship at once came up to him and he was told he could go no further. Captain Vian said, "Are you aware that the *Altmark* is a prison-ship, carrying nearly three hundred British prisoners?"

The senior Norwegian officer stonily replied that the *Altmark* had been examined the previous day, that he knew nothing of any prisoners being aboard, and his orders were to see that she sailed through Norwegian waters unmolested. He also stated that the German ship was unarmed, though it should have been apparent to him that this was not true. He was an officer with his orders, however, and would not deviate in the least from the instructions given him.

Captain Vian recognised the man's resolution and withdrew again. Now again he made a report to London and asked for instructions. Perhaps by now the Cabinet had realised that the diplomatic battle was lost and they must employ other methods to save the prisoners. An instruction was accordingly sent to Captain Vian by Mr. Churchill with the assent of the Cabinet. It is reputed to be brief and Churchillian, and was said to consist of five words only – "Go in and get them."

Five words but to the British sailors, anxious for the safety of their countrymen, they made all the difference. At once the situation was changed – the Navy suddenly felt on top again.

But it wasn't going to be easy. By now it was dark, though a silvery moon lit up the snowy mountains – and left the fiord in the deepest shadow. Usually a pilot was employed to take vessels inside the fiord, but the Navy wasn't going to wait for any pilot even though none of the *Cossack*'s crew had ever sailed into the Josing Fiord before.

Captain Vian ordered a boarding party to make ready under Lieutenant-Commander B.T. Turner, then he put the *Cossack* into the fiord. He ordered his searchlights to be put on, and they came into the fiord behind intensely bright shafts of light that soon revealed the *Altmark*.

At once the Norwegian warships came across and demanded to know what Vian was up to. He told them flatly, "I'm going in to search the *Altmark*." The gloves were off now, and sovereign rights forgotten. No one was going to run British prisoners off under the nose of the Navy.

There was an objection from the Norwegian, but Vian was not in a mood to argue. He said that if the Norwegians liked they could make up a mixed boarding party, but in any event he was going in.

At that the Norwegian commander said he would come aboard the *Cossack* and go with the boarding party; but at the last minute he changed his mind and stayed all during the raid aboard the British destroyer.

The fiord, silent for so long, was suddenly noisy with the shouts of men, the ring of orders, and the noise as the *Altmark* started her engines when she saw the *Cossack*, searchlights blinding the eyes of the Germans, bearing in upon her. It was a tense moment, a time of high drama. The British sailors expected the *Altmark* to jump into action with her armament, but instead, as if still unwilling to violate Norway's so far benevolent neutrality, Captain Dau merely tried to ram the destroyer. Vian managed to avoid the German, though in the confines of the fiord there was little room for manœuvring, and got the bows of the *Cossack* alongside the stern of the prison-ship.

It was a stirring moment, something in the old tradition of the navy. With a yell, Lieutenant-Commander Turner took a flying leap on to the German ship, followed by thirty men from the *Cossack*, armed to the proverbial teeth. A line was got across and the two ships secured together.

There were a hundred and fifty-seven Germans aboard the *Altmark*, about twenty of them from the *Graf Spee*, but the swiftness and audacity of the attack seemed to demoralise them. They were armed, but for a little while did not use their guns.

Then opposition developed and there was firing. The first man to be hit was a warrant officer from the *Cossack*, who was seriously wounded. The small boarding party pitched in to the Germans with their fists, or used their guns as clubs, and the enemy was forced back.

Now British sailors ran through the ship, trying to find the prisoners. Here there were further encounters with the German crew who had started to use their guns. The fights were brief but bloody.

Turner found Captain Dau on the bridge. The *Altmark* had gone aground. Dau admitted he had prisoners aboard, and at once was placed under arrest, a British seaman standing guard over him with a rifle and bayonet. Turner now demanded the keys of the holds in which the prisoners were, but secured no help and the keys could not be found.

Down below, jolted out of an unhappy sleep as the *Altmark* tried to ram the *Cossack*, the prisoners suddenly realised that a bold attempt at rescue was about to be made. At once they leapt to their feet and listened, and then one of the officers got to a spyhole and began to shout the news. There was a searchlight outside – ships approaching. They heard him yell, "We are going to be rescued," and then there was the crash as the *Cossack* and *Altmark* came together.

Suddenly the lights went out, and they heard shots and the sounds of vicious fighting above. And then – in a beautiful moment for the prisoners – a hatch cover was forced off and they heard someone shout, "Are there any English down there?"

There was an instant roar from below and the prisoners began to crowd forward. And then came that now historic cry – "The Navy's here! Come on deck!"

The Navy's here. ... At that, there was a tremendous cheer from the prisoners, and then in a flood they came surging on deck, shaking the hands of the sailors whose dash and gallantry had saved them.

But the fighting was not over. The *Altmark*'s men were taking to the boats. Some got ashore and began to fire upon the *Cossack*, wounding some of the crew. Heavy fire was instantly returned, and in the ensuing battle, until all the prisoners were got on board the *Cossack*, six Germans were killed and many others wounded. An infuriated Berlin, cheated at the last moment of its victory parade of prisoners, made much of these "brutal murders",but the fact is recorded that the first acts of aggression were by the Germans themselves.

Another German boat crashed as others of the *Altmark*'s crew tried to get away in it, and one of the men fell into the icy cold fiord. A British officer dived in and hauled him out, a brave rescue under the circumstances, but unavailing because shortly afterwards the man died.

It was the end of the *Altmark* incident: the true end to the cruise of the *Graf Spee*. There were diplomatic wranglings about the rights and wrongs of the procedure, but to 299 men it didn't mean a thing. They were tearing across the North Sea towards the Scottish port of Leith, uncomfortably crowded aboard a British destroyer, but after all their months of worry and anxiety, they hadn't a care in the world now. They were going home. ...

Home to a war-time Britain, to a brief but joyous reunion with their families. Then back to sea again, to sail the ships that their country so vitally needed to keep her alive – to risk the perils of the oceans with submarine packs beginning to gather, to suffer and sometimes to die as merchant seamen always die when nations go to war.

But that is the lot of the men who choose the sea for their livelihood – a hard life and a dangerous one. Yet somehow Britain always finds the men for her ships in her hours of desperate need.

Appendix

THE BATTLE OF THE RIVER PLATE
13 December 1939

THE RIVER PLATE BATTLE

The following Despatch was submitted to the Lords Commissioners of the Admiralty on the 30th December, 1939, by Rear Admiral H.H. Harwood, K.C.B., O.B.E., Rear Admiral Commanding South American Division:-

H.M.S. AJAX,

30th December, 1939.

I have the honour to submit the following report of the action between H.M. Ships AJAX* (Captain C.H.L. Woodhouse, Royal Navy), ACHILLES† (Captain W.E. Parry, Royal Navy) and EXETER (Captain F.S. Bell, Royal Navy), under my orders, and the German Armoured Ship ADMIRAL GRAF SPEE on Wednesday, 13th December, 1939, and the sequence of events leading to her self-destruction on Sunday, 17th December, 1939.

All times throughout this report are in the time of Zone plus 2, except where otherwise stated.

*Wearing the Broad Pendant of the Commodore Commanding the South American Division.
† Of the New Zealand Division of the Royal Navy.

APPENDIX

PRELIMINARY DISPOSITIONS

2. The British ship DORIC STAR had reported being attacked by a pocket battleship in position 19 degrees 15' south, 5 degrees 5' east during the afternoon of 2nd December, 1939, and a similar report had been sent by an unknown vessel 170 miles south-west of that position at 0500 G.M.T. on 3rd December.
From this data I estimated that at a cruising speed of 15 knots the raider could reach the Rio de Janeiro focal area a.m. 12th December, the River Plate focal area p.m. 12th December or a.m. 13th December and the Falkland Islands area 14th December.

3. I decided that the Plate, with its larger number of ships and its very valuable grain and meat trade, was the vital area to be defended. I therefore arranged to concentrate there my available forces in advance of the time at which, it was anticipated the raider might start operations in that area.

4. In order to bring this about, I made the following signal to the South American Division timed 1315 of 3rd December, 1939:-
"In view of report pocket battleship, amend previous dispositions. CUMBERLAND self-refit at Falkland Islands as previously arranged but keep at short notice on two shafts. ACHILLES leave Rio de Janeiro area so as to arrive and fuel Montevideo 0600 (Zone plus 2) 8th December, EXETER leave Falkland Islands, for Plate a.m. 9th December, covering S.S. LAFONIA with returning volunteers. AJAX, ACHILLES concentrate in position 35 degrees south, 50 degrees west at 1600 (Zone plus 2) 10th December. EXETER to pass through position 090 degrees Medanos Light 150 miles at 0700 12th December. If concentration with AJAX and ACHILLES is not

170

effected by that time further instructions will be issued to EXETER. Oiler OLYNTHUS is to remain at sea rendezvous until situation clears instead of proceeding to Falkland Islands."

5. Strict W/T silence was kept after passing this signal.

6. Concentration of all three ships was effected by 0700 Tuesday, 12th December, and I then proceeded towards position 32 degrees south, 47 degrees west. This position was chosen from my Shipping Plot as being at that time the most congested part of the diverted shipping routes, i.e., the point where I estimated that a raider could do most damage to British shipping.

7. On concentrating I made the following signal timed 1200/12th December to my Force:-
"My policy with three cruisers in company versus one pocket battleship. Attack at once by day or night. By day act as two units, 1st Division (AJAX and ACHILLES) and EXETER diverged to permit flank marking. First Division will concentrate gunfire. By night ships will normally remain in company in open order. Be prepared for the signal ZMM* which is to have the same meaning as MM³ except that for Division read Single Ship."

8. I amplified this later in my signal 1813/12th December as follows:-
"My object in the signal ZMM is to avoid torpedoes and take the enemy by surprise and cross his stern. Without further orders ships are to clear the line of fire by hauling astern of the new leading ship. The new leading ship is to lead the line without further orders so as to maintain decisive gun range."
I exercised this manoeuvre during the evening of 12th December.

THE ACTION

Wednesday, 13th December, 1939
0530-0623.

9. At 0520 / 13th December, the Squadron was in position 34 degrees 34' south, 49 degrees 17' west. With the last of the dawn I exercised manoeuvring signals, and then re-formed the squadron on a course of 060 speed 14 knots in the order AJAX, ACHILLES, EXETER. At 0614, smoke was sighted bearing 320 and EXETER was ordered to close and investigate it. At 0616 EXETER reported "I think it is a pocket battleship" and two minutes later the enemy opened fire, one 11-in. turret at EXETER and the other at AJAX.

10. The First Division immediately altered course together by signal to 340 degrees to close the range. Captain F.S. Bell, Royal Navy, of H.M.S. EXETER, hauled out of the line and altered course to the westward in accordance with my plan, in order to attack the enemy from a widely different bearing and permit flank marking. All ships increased speed.
EXETER opened fire at 0620, ARCHILLES at 0621 and AJAX at 0623.
An enemy report was immediately initiated and was broadcast at 0634. Amplifying reports were made at 0640, 0646 and 0722.

11. From this point until the action was broken off, no alter course signals were made. Captain W.E. Parry, Royal Navy, of H.M.S. ACHILLES manoeuvred his ship as necessary to clear her line of fire, remaining close to AJAX and conforming to her movements. EXETER proceeded independently, her initial course being about 280 degrees.

APPENDIX

I2. AJAX and ACHILLES opened in Single Ship firing, but Concentration was employed as soon as W/T touch had been established at about 0625.

I3. It appeared at this stage as if the enemy was undecided as to her gunnery policy. Her turrets were working under different controls, and she shifted target several times before eventually concentrating both turrets on EXETER.

0623-0630.

I4. EXETER was straddled by GRAF SPEE's third salvo, one shell of which burst short amidships, killed the starboard tube's crew, damaged communications and riddled the searchlights and aircraft. Preparations were being made at this time for catapulting the aircraft, but as both were by then out of action, they were manhandled over the side.

I5. At 0624, after EXETER had fired eight salvos, she received a direct hit from an II-in. direct-action shell on the front of "B" turret. This shell burst on impact, put the turret out of action, and splinters swept the bridge, killing or wounding all personnel there with the exception of the Captain and two others, and wrecked the wheelhouse communications.

I6. Captain F.S. Bell, Royal Navy, then decided to fight his ship from the after conning position, but owing to communications being destroyed it was some time before the ship could be brought under the control of that position, and then it could only be done by means of a chain of messengers to pass orders to the after steering position.
Meanwhile EXETER had swung to starboard, and was closing her "A" arcs,† but she was brought back to port by an order from the torpedo officer, Lieutenant-Commander C.J. Smith,

Royal Navy, who succeeded in getting word through to the lower conning position.

Two more II in. hits were received in the fore part of the ship during this phase.

I7. AJAX and ACHILLES were in Concentration firing and seemed to be making good shooting. They were closing the range rapidly and gaining bearing on the enemy.

0630-0638.

I8. About this time, the GRAF SPEE shifted the fire of one II in. turret on to the First Division and AJAX was straddled three times at about 063I. The First Division turned slightly away to throw out the enemy's gunfire.

His secondary armament was firing alternately at AJAX and ACHILLES, but with no effect, though some salvos fell close.

I9. AJAX catapulted her aircraft with Lieutenant E.D.G. Lewin, Royal Navy, as pilot, at 0637, a very fine evolution observing that "X" and "Y" turrets were at that time firing on a forward bearing. Owing to delay in establishing W/T communication the first air spotting report was not received until 0654. This method was then employed for the rest of the action.

20. The First Division turned back to port at 0634 in order to close the range.

2I. EXETER fired her starboard torpedoes in local control at 0632 as she turned back to her westerly course, but at 0637 the GRAF SPEE altered course some I50 degrees to port, and steered to the north-westward under cover of smoke. AJAX and ACHILLES immediately hauled round, first to north, then to the west to close the range and regain bearing, accepting the temporary loss of "A" arcs. Both ships were by this time proceeding at full speed.

It appears probable that the First Division's concentration and also EXETER'S fire had up to this point been most effective and it is thought that this and the firing of EXETER'S torpedoes were the cause of the enemy making smoke and altering course away.

0638-0650.

22. At about 0638 EXETER altered course to starboard so as to fire her port torpedoes. She then steered to the north-east to close the First Division till about 0645 when she turned to a westerly course to keep within range.

23. During this period, EXETER received two more II in. hits. "A" turret was put out of action, and the second shell burst in the Chief Petty Officers' flat amidships, started a fierce fire, and caused the 4 in. magazine to be flooded by burst water mains. All compass repeaters were now out of action, and Captain Bell, using a boat's compass, resolutely maintained EXETER in action with "Y" turret firing in local control and the gunnery officer, Lieutenant-Commander R.B. Jennings, Royal Navy, controlling the fire from the after searchlight platform.

24. At 0640 an II in. direct action shell fell short of ACHILLES in line with the bridge and burst on the water. Splinters killed four ratings in the D.C.T. and stunned the gunnery officer, Lieutenant R.E. Washbourn, Royal Navy. Captain Parry and the Chief Yeoman who were on the bridge were also slightly wounded at the time. The D.C.T. itself was undamaged and, after a few minutes, resumed control from the after control position which had temporarily taken over. The survivors of

the crew of the D.C.T. took over the duties of the casualties in a most resolute and efficient manner.

About 0646 reception on ACHILLES fire control W/T set faded, and thereafter she carried on in individual control.

0650-0708.

25. During the period ACHILLES was in individual control, she had great difficulty in finding the line, and at first her salvos were falling well short. Reports of the fall of these salvos were transmitted by the aircraft of AJAX whose gun control officer, not knowing that ACHILLES was no longer in concentration firing, accepted them as referring to his own fall of shot, and corrected accordingly.

The enemy was making smoke at the time, and conditions for direct observations were very bad.

This resulted in AJAX salvos falling well over and the target was not found again until 0708.

26. AJAX and ACHILLES hauled round to the north-westward at 0656 to open their "A" arcs. GRAF SPEE made frequent alterations of course to throw out our gunfire, and from 0700 onwards she made great use of smoke; she appeared to have some form of Chloro-sulphonic apparatus aft, and used this as well as smoke floats.

27. Captain Bell, of H.M.S. EXETER, hauled round to the westward at 0650, and was still engaging the enemy, adjusting his course so as to keep "Y" turret bearing.

EXETER now had a list of 7 degrees to starboard, and had several compartments flooded forward as a result of an II in. hit under the forecastle. She was still being engaged by GRAF SPEE, but the latter's fire appeared at this time to be falling a considerable distance over EXETER.

0708-0728.

28. GRAF SPEE'S range from the First Division was still I6,000 yards at 07I0. I then decided to accept the loss of "A" arcs in order to close the range as rapidly as possible. Course was altered to the westward, and AJAX and ACHILLES were ordered to proceed at their utmost speed.

29. At 07I6, GRAF SPEE made a drastic alteration of course to port under cover of smoke, but four minutes later she turned to the north-west and opened her "A" arcs on the First Division. AJAX was immediately straddled three times by II in. at a range of II,000 yards, but the enemy's secondary armament was firing raggedly, and appeared to be going consistently over, between AJAX and ACHILLES.

30. At 0720, the First Division turned to starboard to bring all guns to bear. Our shooting appeared to be very effective, and a fire was observed amidships in GRAF SPEE.

3I. At 0725, AJAX received an II in. delay action hit on the after superstructure. The shell passed through various cabins, then "X" turret trunk, wrecking the turret machinery below the gunhouse and finally bursting in the Commodore's sleeping cabin, doing considerable damage. A portion of the base of the Shell struck "Y" barbette close to the training rack and jammed the turret. It was this shell that killed four and wounded six of "X" turret's crew. This one hit therefore put both "X" and "Y" turrets of AJAX out of action.

32. It now appeared to me that GRAF SPEE intended to neglect EXETER and was determined to close the First Division on a north-westerly course. Thinking she would hold this course, it was decided to fire one broadside of torpedoes from AJAX.

APPENDIX

At 0724 AJAX turned to starboard and fired four torpedoes at
a range of 9,000 yards. GRAF SPEE probably saw these being
fired, as she at once turned some 130 degrees to port, though
she came back to the north-west three minutes later.

0728-0740.

33. EXETER had been dropping gradually astern, as she had
to reduce speed owing to damage forward. She still continued
firing "Y" turret in local control until about 0730, when power
to the turret failed due to flooding. She could then no longer
keep up with the action, and about 0740 steered to the
southeast at slow speed, starting to repair damage and make
herself seaworthy.

34. AJAX and ACHILLES hauled back to about 260 degrees
at 0728 to close the range still further. At 0731, the aircraft
reported "Torpedoes approaching, they will pass ahead of
you." I decided, however, not to take any chances, and altered
course to 180 degrees, engaging the enemy on the starboard
side, with the range closing rapidly. So as to blank ACHILLES'
fire for as short a time as possible, I directed her by signal to
pass under the stern of AJAX.

35. At 0732 GRAF SPEE turned away to the west, making
much smoke and zigzagging to throw out the First Division's
gunfire, which, particularly from ACHILLES, appeared to be
very accurate at this stage. AJAX was also making very good
use of her three available guns. GRAF SPEE altered to the
south-west at 0736, and again brought all guns to bear on the
First Division.

36. By 0738 the range was down to 8,000 yards. At this time I
received a report that AJAX had only 20 per cent, of
ammunition left and had only three guns in action, as one of

the hoists had failed in "B" turret and "X" and "Y" turrets were both out of action.

GRAF SPEE'S shooting was still very accurate and she did not appear to have suffered much damage.

I therefore decided to break off the day action and try and close in again after dark. Accordingly at 0740 AJAX and ACHILLES turned away to the east under cover of smoke.

37. One of GRAF SPEE'S last salvos brought down AJAX'S main top mast and destroyed all her aerials. Jury aerials were, however, soon rigged.

38. It subsequently transpired that the report of shortage of ammunition in AJAX referred only to "A" turret, which had been firing continuously for 8I minutes, but this was not realised at the time.

39. GRAF SPEE made no attempt to follow, but steadied on a course of about 270 degrees, proceeding at about 22 knots on a course direct for the River Plate.

40. After opening the range under smoke for six minutes, I again turned the First Division to the westward and ordered ACHILLES to shadow in Sector "A", on the enemy's starboard quarter, and AJAX in Sector "B", on his port quarter. The range at this time being about I5 miles.

4I. The general trend of GRAF SPEE'S retreat at this stage was about 255 degrees. His very conspicuous control tower made it an easy matter to shadow him at long range in the excellent visibility prevailing.

At 0807, as AJAX'S aerials were still down, I ordered ACHILLES to broadcast GRAF SPEE'S position, course and speed to all British merchant ships. A similar message was broadcast every hour from AJAX until the end of the chase. I also passed this information to Admiralty at 1017 and 1700.

42. At 0912, AJAX recovered her aircraft, the operation being excellently performed under difficult conditions by Captain C.H.L. Woodhouse, and the pilot of the aircraft, Lieutenant E.D.G. Lewin, Royal Navy, and shadowing was resumed.

43. At 0946 I ordered CUMBERLAND, then at the Falkland Islands, to close the Plate at full speed. She left at 1200, on the initiative of her Commanding Officer, Captain W.H.G. Fallowfield, Royal Navy, who had by then only received very jumbled messages. On receipt of my signal she at once increased to full speed.
At 1005 ACHILLES over-estimating the enemy's speed had closed to 23,000 yards. GRAF SPEE thereupon altered course and fired two three gun salvos at ACHILLES; the first was very short, but the second fell close alongside. She appeared to wait for the first salvo to fall before firing the second.
ACHILLES turned away at full speed under smoke and resumed shadowing at longer range.

44. At 1104 a merchant ship was sighted close to GRAF SPEE. She was stopped and was blowing off steam. A few minutes later the following W/T signal was received on 500 k/cs: AJAX (pre-war call sign) from GRAF SPEE – "please pick up lifeboats of English steamer." On coming up with the merchant ship she turned out to be the British S.S. SHAKESPEARE. All her boats were hoisted, and in response to any signals she reported that she was quite all right and did not require any assistance. By this time she was moving out to the southern flank.
At 1105 I received a signal from EXETER who reported that all her turrets were out of action and that she was flooded forward up to No. 14 bulkhead but could still do 18 knots. I ordered her to proceed to the Falkland Islands at whatever

speed was possible without straining her bulkheads. She later reported that one gun of "Y" turret could be fired in local control.

At I347 I informed the British Naval Attache Buenos Aires, that GRAF SPEE was heading direct for the Plate.

45. At I543 ACHILLES signalled "Enemy in sight 297", and later reported "Suspected 8 inch cruiser." However, at I559, she negatived the report, and the ship sighted was subsequently identified as S.S. DELANE, whose streamlined funnel gave her a similar appearance to a "Blucher" at very long range.

46. Shadowing continued without incident until I9I5, when GRAF SPEE altered course and fired two salvos at AJAX who immediately turned away under smoke. The first salvo fell short and in line, the second in AJAX'S wake as she turned. The range at this time was about 26,000 yards.

47. It now appeared that GRAF SPEE intended to enter the Plate, and at I902 I ordered ACHILLES to follow her if she went west of Lobos, while AJAX would proceed south of the English Bank in case she doubled back that way. I also directed ACHILLES to take every advantage of territorial waters while shadowing. My instructions were perfectly carried out by Captain W.E. Parry who took ACHILLES inside Lobos Island and close to the Uruguayan coast.

48. Just after sunset GRAF SPEE fired three salvos at ACHILLES, the third being very close. ACHILLES replied with five salvos and appeared to straddle. ACHILLES at this time was just clear of Punta Negra.

49. The Uruguayan gunboat URUGUAY closed AJAX about 2II5. She appeared to be on patrol duty, but was soon left astern.

50. GRAF SPEE also fired single salvos at ACHILLES at 2132, 2140 and 2143, but the visibility to the eastward was very bad for her at these times and firing must have merely been intended to keep shadowers at a distance.

51. Those shots, however, did not deter Captain Parry from keeping touch and by 2200 ACHILLES had closed to within five miles of GRAF SPEE. The latter was well silhouetted first against the afterglow, and then against the lights of Montevideo. GRAF SPEE proceeded north of the English Bank and anchored in Montevideo roads at 0050.

52. My chief pre-occupation at that time was how long did GRAF SPEE intend to stay there. The primary necessity was to keep to seaward of the GRAF SPEE if she came to sea again, and at the same time to avoid being caught against the dawn light. At 2350 I ordered AJAX and ACHILLES to withdraw from the Plate, ACHILLES to patrol the area from the Uruguayan coast to a line 120 degrees from English Bank, and AJAX the southern area, both ships to move back into the Plate in their respective sectors after dawn.

Thursday, 14th December.

53. I requested His Britannic Majesty's Minister, Montevideo, to use every possible means of delaying GRAF SPEE's sailing, in order to gain time for reinforcements to reach me. I suggested that he should sail British ships and invoke the 24-hour rule to prevent her leaving.

54. I learned that ARK ROYAL, RENOWN, NEPTUNE, DORSETSHIRE, SHROPSHIRE and three destroyers were all closing the Plate, but none of them could reach me for at least five days.

55. CUMBERLAND reported that she would arrive in the Plate at 2200/14th December, having made the passage from the Falkland Islands in 34 hours. I ordered her to cover the sector between Rouen and English Banks, with ACHILLES to the north of her and AJAX to the south. These dispositions were maintained during the night of the 14th/15th December. Should GRAF SPEE come out, she was to be shadowed and all ships were to concentrate sufficiently far to seaward to enable a concerted attack to be carried out.

Friday, 15th December.

56. I ordered R.F.A. OLYNTHUS, Captain L.N. Hill, to proceed to Rouen Bank to be ready to fuel H.M. ships, and proceeded there in AJAX. I ordered CUMBERLAND to close and cover AJAX, remaining at visibility distance to the northward so as to be able to give warning in case GRAF SPEE came out without her sailing being reported.

57. I made the following policy signal timed 1135/15th December:-
"My object destruction. Necessitates concentrating our forces. Increased risk of enemy escape accepted. ACHILLES is now to watch north of English Bank and CUMBERLAND to west of English Bank, latter showing herself off Montevideo in daylight. If enemy leaves before 2100, ships in touch shadow at maximum range – all units concentrate on shadower. If enemy has not left by 2100, leave patrol positions and concentrate in position 090 degrees San Antonio 15 miles by 0030; AJAX will probably join CUMBERLAND on her way south.
"If enemy leaves Montevideo after sunset, CUMBERLAND is at once to fly off one aircraft to locate and shadow enemy, if necessary landing in a lee, risking internment, and trying

to find a British ship in the morning. If plan miscarries, adopt plan "B", all units concentrate in position 36 degrees south, 52 degrees west at 0600."

I also repeated my signal I200/I2th December (see paragraph 7) to CUMBERLAND at II36/I5th December, substituting CUMBERLAND for EXETER in the original.

58. AJAX took in 200 tons of fuel from OLYNTHUS, bad weather causing wires to part including the spans of two hurricane hawsers. AJAX then proceeded to join CUMBERLAND.

59. I received a report that GRAF SPEE had landed a funeral party this morning, and later, that she had been granted an extension of her stay up to 72 hours, in order to make herself seaworthy. It appeared that she had been damaged far more extensively than I had thought likely, and had been hit 60 to 70 times in all. The British ship ASHWORTH was sailed at I900 and GRAF SPEE accepted the edict that she would not be allowed to sail for 24 hours after this. At the same time I could feel no security that she would not break out at any moment.

Saturday, I6th December.

60. CUMBERLAND, AJAX, and ACHILLES made rendezvous off San Antonio at 0030 in accordance with my plan. The squadron closed the Plate towards dawn and AJAX flew off her aircraft for a reconnaissance of the harbour. The aircraft was instructed not to fly over territorial waters.

6I. The aircraft returned at 0830 and the crew reported that they had been unable to see anything owing to bad visibility. They had been fired at while in the vicinity of the Whistle Buoy. This seemed to indicate that GRAF SPEE was taking advantage of the mist and was trying to break out. All ships went to action stations, but a report received shortly afterwards from Montevideo indicated that GRAF SPEE was still in harbour.

62. I informed H.B.M. Minister, Montevideo, of the firing on our aircraft, and suggested that an investigation into this might be a way of delaying GRAF SPEE sailing. He replied, however, that it was definitely not GRAF SPEE who fired, and that it had possibly been the Argentine Guard Gunboat at Recalada, or in some other position.

63. The Admiralty informed me in message 0219/16th December that I was free to engage GRAF SPEE anywhere outside the three-mile limit. I decided to move my patrol into the area north and east of English Bank, as I considered that a battle in the very restricted water just outside the three-mile limit off Montevideo was impracticable, owing to lack of sea room, and possibility of "overs" landing in Uruguay and causing international complications.

64. Information from Montevideo was to the effect that GRAF SPEE was still repairing damage, having obtained assistance from the shore, and had provisioned. It was reported as unlikely that she would sail that night; on the other hand, once again I did not feel able to rely on such an optimistic report.

65. I signalled the following appreciation to ships in company timed 1615/16th December:- "My object Destruction necessitates keeping my force together. My Appreciation. Rely on getting his time of sailing and initial course from shore. For subsequent movements rely on CUMBERLAND'S aircraft reconnaissance reports.
"Enemy's courses of Action. (a) North of English Bank, (b) Between English and Rouen Banks. (c) Between Rouen Bank and San Antonio. (d) Double back on any track. My Course of

Action. I rule out righting him off Whistle Buoy as being politically impossible. Until the dawn phase I want to keep the advantage of light and from this it follows that I must keep to the east and move to intercept him from area to area depending on time and information. My Plan. To keep within reach of intercepting him north of English Bank moving south or doubling back as information comes in. Tactical. I must keep CUMBERLAND so placed that she will not have her fire masked initially, and therefore I will work in divisions 8 cables apart with ACHILLES in close order astern of AJAX.
"After action commences, divisions have complete freedom of action. CUMBERLAND'S aircraft is to be flown off as soon as news is received of enemy's sailing."

66. The British ship DUNSTER GRANGE was sailed from Montevideo at 1700 and a further period before GRAF SPEE could be allowed to sail was claimed. It was, however, reported that she had made very rapid progress with her repairs, and might break out at any moment.

67. The difficulty of intercepting GRAF SPEE who had so many courses of action open to her will, I feel sure, be realised. It was in the dog watches of this evening that I received the Naval Secretary's signal 1717/16th December informing me from the First Lord of the Admiralty of the honours so graciously bestowed by His Majesty the King on myself, Captain W.E. Parry, Captain C.H.L. Woodhouse and Captain F.S. Bell, and also that I had been promoted to Rear Admiral to date 13th December. This was a most stimulating tonic to us all and I took steps to pass it on to H.M. Ships under my command, emphasising the share of all concerned in the honours which their senior officers had received.

68. The squadron spent the night patrolling on a north and

south line five miles to the east of the English Bank Light Buoy. OLYNTHUS proceeded to sea with order to be at the Rouen Bank by I000 the next morning if GRAF SPEE had not broken out.

Sunday, I7th December.

69. I ordered ACHILLES who was getting low in fuel, to oil from OLYNTHUS off the Rouen Bank during the forenoon. AJAX and CUMBERLAND acted as look-outs at visibility distance during the operation. The squadron then cruised in company off the south-east of the English Bank, remaining concentrated throughout the afternoon and ready again to take up the same night patrol as on the previous night.

70. It was reported that GRAF SPEE had landed all her borrowed welding apparatus during this forenoon. We all expected that she would break out at any moment. I would like to place on record the fact that at this stage the most cheerful optimism pervaded all ships in spite of the fact that this was the fifth night of waiting for the enemy.

7I. At 1540 I received a signal that GRAF SPEE was transferring between 300 and 400 men to the German ship TACOMA lying close to her in the ante-port. At I720, a further report stated that over 700 men with their baggage and some provisions had now been transferred, and that there were indications that GRAF SPEE intended to scuttle herself. Shortly after this GRAF SPEE was reported as weighing.

72. I immediately altered course to close the Whistle Buoy, and increased to 25 knots. AJAX'S aircraft was flown off and ordered to proceed towards Montevideo and report the position of GRAF SPEE and also TACOMA.

GRAF SPEE left harbour at 1815 and proceeded slowly to the westward. TACOMA also weighed, and followed her out of harbour.

73. I ordered my squadron to assume the First Degree of Readiness, in case GRAF SPEE intended re-transferring her crew from TACOMA outside the harbour, or intended to break out with or without her surplus crew.

74. AJAX aircraft reported sighting GRAF SPEE in a position in shallow water some six miles south-west of Montevideo. At 2054 the aircraft signalled: "GRAF SPEE has blown herself up."

75. The squadron carried on towards Montevideo, proceeding north of the English Bank, AJAX and ACHILLES cheering ship as they passed each other.

76. Once again Captain Woodhouse and Lieutenant Lewin made an excellent recovery of AJAX's aircraft, this time under almost dark conditions.
Navigation lights were then switched on and the squadron steamed past the Whistle Buoy within about four miles of the wreck of the GRAF SPEE. It was now dark, and she was ablaze from end to end, flames reaching almost as high as the top of her control tower, a magnificent and most cheering sight.

REMARKS BY REAR ADMIRAL COMMANDING SOUTH AMERICA DIVISION
Appreciation of conduct of Commanding Officers and Ships' Companies.

77. I have the greatest pleasure in informing you of the very high standard of efficiency and courage that was displayed

by all officers and men throughout the five days of the operation under review.

78. Captain W.E. Parry, Royal Navy, of H.M.S. ACHILLES; Captain C.H.L. Woodhouse, Royal Navy, of H.M.S. AJAX; and Captain F.S. Bell, Royal Navy, of H.M.S. EXETER, all handled their ships in a most efficient and resolute manner.

79. In addition I would like to place on record the very great assistance that I received throughout this period from my Flag Captain and Chief Staff Officer, Captain C.H.L. Woodhouse, Royal Navy.

80. The speedy arrival of H.M.S. CUMBERLAND, Captain W.H.G. Fallowfield, Royal Navy, from the Falkland Islands, was a most creditable performance, especially as that ship was self-refitting at the time the action commenced.

8I. Throughout the days of waiting off the Plate, R.F.A. OLYNTHUS, Captain L.N. Hill, arrived punctually at the various rendezvous given him and did everything possible to facilitate the refuelling of H.M. Ships.

82. Within my own knowledge, and from the reports of the Commanding Officers there are many stories of bravery, devotion to duty and of the utmost efficiency which shows that H.M. Ships have been forcefully trained and made thoroughly ready to deal with the many and various exigencies of battle. In accordance with Admiralty message I755/I6th December, I am submitting separately a list of officers and ratings whom I consider to be especially deserving of award. I would remark, however, that the standard throughout has been so high that the preparation of this list has been very difficult.

APPENDIX

83. I would like also to place on record the honour and pleasure I had to taking one of H.M. Ships of the New Zealand Division into action, and fully concur with the Commanding Officer of H.M.S. ACHILLES in paragraph 27 of his report where he remarks that "New Zealand has every reason to be proud of her seamen during their baptism of fire."

84. Further, it is most satisfactory for me to be able to inform you that the machinery and equipment generally of H.M. Ships proved to be of the highest efficiency and well able to stand up to the prolonged strain of battle.

Lessons learned.

85. The main impression left on my mind is of the adequacy of our peace training. Little that had not been practised occurred, particularly among the repair parties. Nevertheless, there are a very large number of points brought out in the reports by the Commanding Officers and I would recommend that they should be carefully studied.

86. As soon as the three ships were in company at the Falkland Islands I ordered committees of the Gunnery, Torpedo and Engineer Officers to be formed so as to analyse the lessons learned. Their conclusions have been forwarded direct to Admiralty.

Enemy Tactics.

87. The most salient point is that GRAF SPEE closed on sighting us, firing one turret at First Division and the other at EXETER.
This initial closing of the range by the enemy had the effect of bringing both the 8 in. and 6 in. cruisers into effective gun

range at once and so avoided for us the most difficult problem of gaining range in the face of II in. gunfire.

88. It would appear that GRAF SPEE was heavily handled by the gunfire both of the First Division's concentration and also by that of EXETER in the initial phase, the culminating perhaps being the firing of torpedoes by H.M.S. EXETER. At this point GRAF SPEE turned away under smoke and from that time onwards her Commanding Officer displayed little offensive spirit and did not take advantage of the opportunity that was always present either to close the First Division or EXETER, the latter – and he must have known it – only having one turret in action. Instead GRAF SPEE retired between the two and allowed herself to be fired at from both flanks. Only at one period, i.e., at 0720, did she again open her "A" arcs and concentrate on the First Division, and she immediately abandoned this when AJAX fired torpedoes.

89. Her frequent alterations of course under smoke were, from an avoiding action point of view, well carried out and undoubtedly threw out our gunfire. This has shown up the necessity for more frequent practice at a highly mobile target at fine angles of inclination. GRAF SPEE had an exceptionally high degree of manoeuvrability and apparently used full wheel for her turns. On many occasions this gave her an apparent list which raised our hopes, but she always came upright again on steadying.

90. At no time did GRAF SPEE steam at a higher speed than 24 knots, and generally her speed was between I9 and 22 knots. It was noticed that from the time of first sighting she was making a considerable amount of reddish-brown and occasionally white smoke.

9I. Enemy smoke screens were good but not entirely effective as they did not rise high enough. A point brought out was the necessity for remote control of our smoke floats. Endeavours to light ours while the main armament was firing presented many difficulties.

Enemy Gunnery.

92. GRAF SPEE'S II in. fire was accurate throughout, particularly for line. The rate of fire was slow and there were short periods in which either one or the other turret did not appear to be firing, but by the evening phase both turrets were in action. They certainly did excellent shooting at AJAX and ACHILLES at a range of about 26,000 yards while these ships were shadowing. It was evident from this that shadowing ships should, available speed permitting, zigzag so as to prevent too accurate range plotting by the enemy. It was also found desirable to make drastic alterations of course when the first salvo was fired.

93. Perhaps the most interesting point was the mixing of armour-piercing delay action projectiles and direct action. AJAX'S one II in. hit and several of EXETER'S were of the delay action type. A delay of 42 feet was measured in AJAX and 65 feet in EXETER. It was most noticeable that at the short range at which the action was fought the II in. projectiles proceeded more or less on a horizontal course through the ship and did not directly affect the vitals below.

94. The direct action type produced most serious, and to a certain extent unexpected results. They burst on impact with either the ship or the water and showered splinters in all directions, causing a very large number of casualties to personnel and damage to rigging, electric cables and material generally. I would stress the necessity for more protection of bridges, fire control cables and such important parts of the offensive organisation as the 6 in. director tower. A large

number of casualties on EXETER'S bridge were caused by splinters from the hit on "B" turret ricochetting off the roof of the bridge. Immediate steps should be taken to pad the under surface of bridge roofs.

95. The II in. shells that fell short made a black splash and in the vicinity of bursts a black dust like soot was found.

96. The enemy 6 in. fire was ragged and ineffective and caused little, if any, anxiety.

97. There is some evidence that GRAF SPEE fired time-fuzed H.E. possibly from her high angle guns.
Aircraft.

98. The flying off of AJAX'S aircraft with "X" and "Y" turrets firing on a forward bearing while the aircraft was waiting was a gallant and most resolute effort. The handling of both AJAX and her aircraft during subsequent recoveries was also very well carried out. During the past two months I have been most impressed with the rough weather capabilities of the Seafox type of aircraft.

99. EXETER'S Walrus aircraft had been refuelled for the dawn phase, and it was unfortunate that both were hit by splinters before either could be flown off. It was extremely fortunate that the petrol which was being sprayed all over the after part of the ship did not cause any fires. This danger must always be present when an unexpected encounter occurs. Again it emphasizes the necessity for emptying the aircraft of petrol should a night encounter be likely and for the ability to be able to fuel and defuel quickly.

100. Another point that comes out is the need for speeding up the catapulting process.

I0I. The aircraft, once up, though extremely valuable at times, was not entirely successful.

I02. GRAF SPEE's aircraft was out of action before the battle and did not take part.

Increased Protection.

I03. There must always be a tendency for a cruiser to desire increased protection and most of the claims must, generally speaking, be resisted. Nevertheless, there are portions of the control and of the offensive armament that I feel very strongly should be protected against splinters.

(*a*) The killing or wounding of nearly the whole of EXETER'S bridge personnel is one example. The bullet-proof plating, backed up by the instrument plate was more or less successful in keeping out most of the splinters. It should, however, be made thicker and, as mentioned before, the underside of the bridge roof should be padded to prevent splinters ricochetting off it. It was this latter factor that was the main cause of the casualties.

(*b*) The hitting of ACHILLES director control tower was most unfortunate, and I consider that, particularly in those ships with only one director tower it should be made splinter proof and also that the leads to it should be in a protected tube.

(*c*) The After Conning Position. This position was used throughout most of the action in EXETER, but its communications failed, and Captain Bell had to con the ship through a chain of messengers. In AJAX casualties from splinters occurred in this position, though it appears they were downwards from a hit on the main-topmast. I consider that the after conning position should be protected and more attention paid to the security of its communications.

(*d*) Other exposed personnel liable to attack from, splinters. I consider that the experience of this action shows that some